**Advance P**

M000014809

*Richard Loren's lively and colorful memoir isn't simply a behind-the-curtains look at working with some of rock's biggest names, including the Grateful Dead and The Doors. It's the story of rock 'n' roll itself—how, in the 60s and 70s, the music leapt from the underground to the mainstream, and how young men like Loren were swept up in the madness and magic of it all.*

DAVID BROWNE
ROLLING STONE contributing editor
and author of FIRE and RAIN: THE BEATLES, SIMON & GARFUNKEL, JAMES
TAYLOR, CSNY AND THE LOST STORY OF 1970

*Richard Loren was a witness to one of the most creative and chaotic eras of American musical history. That he lived this life is remarkable; that he wrote his story with such affection, perspective, and insight is impressive. And yes, that he remembers so many details of this long, strange trip is perhaps the most amazing accomplishment of all.* High Notes, *indeed.*

WARREN LEIGHT
Playwright
and author of the Tony-Award-winning play, SIDE MAN

*It was the best of times, it was the worst of times . . . and Richard Loren was there for it all. Fascinating.*

MARTY BALIN
JEFFERSON AIRPLANE founder and lead singer

*[Richard Loren was] one of the best managers we had.*

PHIL LESH
GRATEFUL DEAD bass player
and author of SEARCHING FOR THE SOUND: MY LIFE WITH THE GRATEFUL DEAD

*When the Grateful Dead walked onto the stage in front of the Great Pyramid at Giza—among the highest points of their illustrious ride—they could thank Richard Loren for the trip. His career has lots of other big moments—working with The Doors, Jefferson Airplane, Jerry Garcia and his various side projects—and they're all in High Notes. He was there and he tells it straight. And it's a great story.*

DENNIS MCNALLY
GRATEFUL DEAD publicist and historian
and author of *A LONG STRANGE TRIP: THE INSIDE HISTORY OF THE GRATEFUL DEAD* and *DESOLATE ANGEL: JACK KEROUAC, THE BEAT GENERATION, AND AMERICA*

*Richard Loren's* High Notes *is a fast-paced and bracing plunge into the backstage and offstage world of some of rock's most intriguing rebels, including Jim Morrison and The Doors, Jefferson Airplane, and Jerry Garcia and the Grateful Dead. Loren's clear-eyed and at times funny personal saga takes us on a wild ride that encompasses everything from working with Liberace in his glittering prime to arranging the Dead's transcendent Egypt adventure, with many a strange tale in between and after.*

BLAIR JACKSON
author of *GARCIA: AN AMERICAN LIFE*

*Richard Loren's memoir provides a behind-the-scenes backstage pass to observe him balancing on his unique journey along a musical tightrope between Liberace and the Grateful Dead. Written with insight and revelation,* High Notes *is a treat to read with an afterglow to treasure.*

PAUL KRASSNER
author of *CONFESSIONS OF A RAVING, UNCONFINED NUT: MISADVENTURES IN THE COUNTERCULTURE*

*This witty, generous, intimate, and touching memoir of a rock life is a must-read for all fans of the Grateful Dead, The Doors, Jefferson Airplane, and, yes, Liberace. It's also an inspiring tale of personal transformation. Richard Loren's book is a trip worth taking. Get on board!*

CHARLES LINDHOLM, PhD
PROFESSOR OF ANTHROPOLOGY, Boston University
and author of *CHARISMA*

# HIGH NOTES

## A ROCK MEMOIR

## RICHARD LOREN

WITH STEPHEN ABNEY

East Pond Publishing

DAMARISCOTTA
MAINE

Printed in the United States of America.

Cataloguing-in-Publication data for this book is available from the Library of Congress

East Pond Publishing edition 2014

East Pond Publishing hardback and paperback editions 2014

ISBN 978-0-9709407-1-1 (paperback)

ISBN 978-0-9709407-0-4 (hardcover)

Published by East Pond Publishing, Damariscotta, Maine
Contact: Sophia Wise at Sophia@eastpondpublishing.com

This is a work of narrative nonfiction. The dialogue in this book is the author's rendition of what was actually said. It is based on actual events, personal conversations, interviews, written accounts, and firsthand knowledge of the characters' states of mind. When possible, the re-created dialogue was reviewed by knowledgeable individuals for accuracy and tone. Names, places, dates, and events are real. Places, names, and events are utilized for descriptive purposes to depict where incidents and events occurred.

The author has made every effort to clear copyright permissions, but where this has not been possible and amendments are required, the publisher will be pleased to make any necessary arrangements at the earliest opportunity.

Editor: Lauren Mosko Bailey

Copy editor: Susan Pink

Proofreader: Debbye Butler

Interior book format: Tim Nason

Book cover and back design: Mark Greenbaum/Greenbomb Studios

Photo: Mark Greenbaum

Tail on my Kite: Deborah Lang

Web design: By Chrein.com/Greenbomb Studios

www.highnotes.org

# Dedication

To the gifted—and revolutionary—rock musicians,
singers, and songwriters of the 60s, 70s, and 80s
who rocked our world, who let us break on through to the
other side, and whose words and music continue to inspire,
enlighten, and entertain.

# CONTENTS

Foreword by David Grisman

Prologue: Bates College, Lewiston, Maine

## PART ONE: NEW YORK CITY

*My life with Jefferson Airplane, The Doors,
and the Chambers Brothers*

## PART TWO: STINSON BEACH, CALIFORNIA

*Davis Grisman, the Rowan Brothers,
Garcia-Saunders, and Old and in the Way*

# PART THREE: THE GRATEFUL DEAD

*Politics, Grateful Dead Movie, Garcia Bands, Egypt,*
*Saturday Night Live, Alaska, and Radio City Music Hall*

# PART FOUR: THE GRATEFUL DEAD
# MERRY-GO-ROUND

*Germany, Mississippi River Boat, Watch the River Flow,*
*Sirens of Titan, and Garcia-Grisman*

Epilogue: Genes, Fate, and Legacy

*Acknowledgments*

*About the Authors*

A ROCK MEMOIR

# FOREWORD

I first met the author of this memoir at the Convention Hall in Asbury Park, New Jersey, in the summer of 1968. He was the new agent for the band I'd formed with Peter Rowan—Earth Opera. I was hiding in the men's room, pretending that nature had called, to buy our band a few more minutes before we had to start warming up the crowd, which was filtering in to see the then-exploding Doors. That night, Richard Loren and I made an immediate and permanent connection (we're still fast friends) despite the fact that he was the "suit" and I was the "artist."

Richard was never a typical anything. Although he was already an experienced music biz hustler with an agenda that night, I could see that beneath his ebullient surface was a true seeker of knowledge and wisdom with just the right dash of cynicism, coupled with a wacky sense of humor (and a love for superior cannabis) that told me that here was a fellow who could simultaneously create and dismiss the bullshit that pervades the entertainment industry, see beyond it, and just plain enjoy the dance of life at any given moment.

Today, nearly half a century after our first encounter, Richard is telling his tale in a most endearing and literate fashion. I enjoyed it thoroughly, and so will you!

David Grisman,
May 2014

# PROLOGUE
# BATES COLLEGE
# LEWISTON, MAINE

"How did you get your start?" Alex Bushe, a nineteen-year-old sophomore, asked me on a December day in 2003.

Alex was a passionate fan of the Grateful Dead and curated an online site that collected and distributed Grateful Dead and other performance tapes. A friend had referred him to me, and we set up a meeting at Bates, a small liberal arts college in Maine, to explore the possibility of a project involving the Dead's musical archives.

"Well," I said after pausing to reflect, "it all began with Liberace."

"Who?"

As I told Alex about some of my diverse experiences in the music business, I realized that they formed a single narrative. As one story led to another, I was overwhelmed thinking about what had transpired. Alex's eagerness to hear more encouraged me to continue, and we chatted for several hours and agreed to meet again.

Talking with Alex inspired me to embark on a memoir project. As I began systematically chronicling the episodes that eventually became the chapters in this book, I discovered that putting my life into perspective chronologically was a detailed, daunting, and demanding task.

Among other things, it rekindled many old emotions connected to the people and events in my past, and was in a way—a spiritual pilgrimage. As I revisited the personalities and places that marked the years, I experienced affection, humility, reconciliation, forgiveness, humor, understanding, and gratitude.

Looking back was as satisfying as it was difficult, and I highly recommend the process as a ritual everyone should endeavor to make. To tell the story of your life in words, songs, pictures, or whatever medium you choose will allow you the opportunity to know yourself in a profoundly affecting way. The process can be a voyage of self-discovery and lead to the peace of reconciliation. Perhaps, just as importantly, it leaves a record for those who follow, a thread that helps to bind the fabric of the passing years.

# PART ONE:

# NEW YORK CITY

*My life with Jefferson Airplane, The Doors,
and the Chambers Brothers*

# CHAPTER 1

## LEE AND ME

What's he really like? Under the veneer of fame, are celebrities really just like us? Is it possible, as Oscar Levant famously questioned, "to cut through the phony tinsel to the real tinsel underneath"?

In the summer of 1966, I was asking myself these questions as I waited for Liberace, the legendary entertainer, to arrive. I was a manager at Music Fair Enterprises in Baltimore, which staged premiere musicals and live performances in a string of large-tent summer venues along the East Coast. As a recent college graduate, this was my first real job in the entertainment business. I was responsible not only for all the technical details, but also for pampering the stars by ensuring that their every need was met. Liberace had contracted to do the final eight shows of the season, and the pressure was on.

Liberace and his entourage were almost an hour late. A local orchestra was tuning up and rehearsing in the tent; I was standing outside, keeping watch for the star's arrival with our press agent and the union reps, who were getting impatient in the oppressive humidity. Finally, three shiny limos rolled up. Liberace's musicians, stage manager, and musical conductor, as well as various other members of the troupe, emerged from the cars. Then, at long last, Liberace appeared, elegantly coiffed and wearing an immaculate white linen suit and a bright floral-print sport shirt. His outfit paled in comparison to his over-the-top stage attire but was far from ordinary street wear on a hot summer afternoon. I had wondered whether I was going to see him in hot pants and knee socks, but now I assumed he was reserving those for his performance. The famous Liberace smile, which inspired an almost religious devotion among his fans, radiated confidence and charm and instantly evaporated the sticky tension.

As we queued up to greet him and shake hands, I was wondering how to address him—"Liberace," "Mr. Liberace," "Your Eminence"? As I introduced myself, he said, "Call me Lee!" With a flash of that five-mile smile, he added, "All my friends do. It's the only thing I answer to—besides 'Hey, Beautiful,' of course."

I would have been happy lingering in the glow of my new friend's charismatic presence, but I felt someone push me aside. As I turned, I saw Blossom Horowitz, a florid woman in her late fifties who was determined to take center stage in the court of The Sun Queen. She was the director of group sales and a real piece of work. Always tan and ostentatiously dressed in resplendent designer finery, she was a nouveau-riche fashion plate. She loved to flaunt what she thought was the importance of her position. In her mind, everyone but the stars was expendable and at the mercy of her every whim. With me out of the way, she marched right up to Liberace, extended her hand, and bent slightly as if expecting a European-style kiss— "Lee, you are *fabulous!*" she gushed. "I've been *dying* to meet you for years!" She introduced herself and announced, "I sold out ALL your shows," as if attracting an audience was all her doing and had nothing to do with Liberace. I peered around her beehive hairdo and dangling gold earrings to see the subtly reduced wattage in his smile, giving away the fact that he was tolerating her as a matter of professional courtesy. "If there's *anything* you need, you come right to me," she babbled on. "Never mind the staff and those young managers!" Her display of self-importance was even more pretentious than her outfit. She clucked on for several more insufferable moments, and then, with the audacity of the fatally clueless, she kissed Liberace on the cheek, curtsied, smiled, did a 180, attempted to swivel her hips, and strutted off trailing vapors of sickly sweet perfume.

I was appalled and embarrassed, but Lee just shrugged and said, "In show business, *everyone* gets to play their role. We have a great tolerance," he smiled, "for people who are different."

## The Pampered Perfectionist

Lee and I strolled around the tent and the dressing room and inspected the ramp that connected the dressing room and the circular stage. Lee would be racing up and down that ramp in the dim backstage light between numbers to do his many costume changes, and we wanted to make sure there were no obstructions that might trip him up.

On stage, Liberace was a perfectionist, and he traveled with his own stage manager and musical director to ensure that local producers met his demanding standards. Off stage, he had demands too. He loved sharing good food with his friends after a show, and his contract included a clause stipulating post-concert dinners. The unenviable task of arranging them fell to me.

At the time, most nightlife in Baltimore consisted of drinking beer and cracking crab at home. Restaurants closed by ten, so late-night dinners required a special request. My first thought was to have catered meals delivered to the theater after each show, but the venue didn't have a pleasant area that could comfortably seat a group, so I quickly dismissed that idea. After brainstorming with the show's press agent, I decided to contact the owner of Baltimore's fashionable Pimlico Restaurant, one of our first choices for visiting celebrity lunches. Its old-fashioned elegance and fine food were always a hit. I presented the idea not as a request but as the honor of hosting after-hour dinners for Liberace, his guests, and a few select members of the press.

The restaurant would have to stay open long after its usual closing time and pay its staff to work overtime, but the owner was shrewd. He saw the offer as an invaluable publicity op, and it was. The positive in-depth coverage by the press, with glowing descriptions of the place, the food, and the host's magnanimous gesture, was the kind of publicity money couldn't buy! I added the icing on the cake by giving the owner six front-row tickets for each of Liberace's eight shows. In return, I enjoyed several complimentary upscale dining experiences at the Pimlico. "Yes. Lee's fine and says hello to everyone at the Pimlico," became a phrase I happily and regularly relayed.

## A Candelabrum in the Wind

On the evening of the first show, I arrived at the tent several hours before the performance and was surprised to see a long line of cars already waiting for the parking lot to open. I had the attendants open the gates and let people file into the theater before the original seating time. As I watched Lee's fans eagerly take their seats, I enjoyed the parade of predominately middle-aged and elderly women, a few with their obviously reluctant husbands in tow. In 1966, The Who were talkin' 'bout "My Generation," The Beatles were blowing minds with "Rubber Soul," and Bob Dylan was pushing the envelope with "Highway 61 Revisited." These bands and others were ushering in a new sound and breaking cultural and musical barriers, but the pop entertainers from the forties and fifties still had their fans, especially in working-class cities such as Baltimore.

Liberace had started out as a conventional piano player in vaudeville and nightclubs in the early forties. As he gained experience and showbiz savvy, he crafted an act that was immensely popular with a unique persona that defied categorization. Rock promoter Bill Graham later said about the Grateful Dead, "The Grateful Dead are not the best at what they do; they are the only ones who do what they do." That too was true of Lee. He was an anomaly in a business that spawned the likes of Mr. Rogers, Tiny Tim, and Truman Capote. Liberace is remembered more for the way he conducted his life and his flamboyant showmanship than for his piano-playing skills. He was a well-trained and highly skilled pianist, but there was no dearth of people who fit that description. He found a way to stand out and earned his well-deserved fame by embellishing his talents with fabulous fashions, genuine charm, and unabashed ostentation. In a way, the piano was just a prop for the spectacle that was Liberace.

Wladziu Valentino Liberace, who was raised in a modest and devoutly Catholic family in Milwaukee, escaped the lower rungs of the entertainment industry by shrewdly melding his midwestern schmaltz and Las Vegas glitter to become the highest-paid entertainer in the world. Walter Busterkeys, as he called himself during his vaudeville days, had learned early in his career that it was more important to put on a show than a concert, and he was a genius at emphasizing lighting, props, and presentation over the music.

On opening night in Baltimore, Lee didn't disappoint. He took the stage in one of his signature over-the-top glittering evening jackets and warmed up the audience by quipping, "Twenty-seven beaded purses died to make this coat!"

When he had everyone chuckling, he sighed and mused, "Nobody likes a show-off!" Then, laying his hands on the piano keys, he added, "But everyone loves a genius!"

He amazed the crowd with a lightning-fast virtuoso version of "Flight of the Bumble Bee," segued into a rollicking "Beer Barrel Polka"—punctuated with some snappy jokes about his beloved Polish family—and completed his first of many sets with a medley of pop favorites. Gershwin's "Rhapsody in Blue" turned into "Embraceable You," then "Swanee," then "I Got Rhythm," and finally, "Twelfth Street Rag" in double time. It was cheesy as all get-out but absolutely dynamic! He captured the audience's energy, made it his own, and dashed off stage to a thunderous round of applause. The stage lights dimmed, but before the crowd could catch its breath, the lights came up to reveal a new, beautiful, and delicately designed set with classic pillars, arches, and dark gauze surrounding his shiny grand piano. A huge crystal chandelier was the only light, and it cast a warm glow over the stage and the orchestra as they struck up a magnificent classical prelude. Suddenly, a light-footed Lee swept onto the stage in a dazzling black-and-rhinestone tuxedo.

His personality morphed from a funny and talented mid-western piano player to a witty and urbane concert pianist playing beautiful renditions of Liszt, Tchaikovsky, and Chopin with full orchestral accompaniment. He managed to take familiar classical pieces and give them his own inimitable treatment, joking, "I only play the best parts!" The evening flew by in a series of outlandish costume changes and stylish sets, highlighting an impish showman who was a musical and theatrical chameleon. But beyond all his gimmicks and disguises, Lee connected with his audience with a warmth and self-satirizing humor that made him seem less a slick celebrity than a favorite son performing before a loving family. His appeal hinged on his ability to maintain the paradox of being cleverly glib and gently genuine simultaneously. He was a master!

After wowing the audience with his fast-paced and perfectly delivered routines, he did several encores and then made his way to the stage door to sign autographs and chat with his fans. Standing off to the side, I could see the smiles on their enraptured faces as they waited for their chance to meet the famous Liberace. That said it all for me.

I overheard a little blue-haired woman, as she extended her playbill for Liberace to autograph, announce, "My friend's husband says you're a homosexual. Is that true?"

Without missing a beat, he replied, "My dear, jealous people will say anything!" He flashed his famous smile. "We don't respond to it. It's beneath us, don't you think?"

"Absolutely!" she nodded. "He's a vulgar man!"

After an hour of luxuriating in the adulation of his devotees, he blew a kiss to the faithful, and I escorted him—and his inner circle—to a waiting white Cadillac limo. He was pleased with the show and his performance as well as the staging and how smoothly things had run. In gratitude, he graciously asked me to join him on the ride to the restaurant. I waited until everyone was seated before I got in. As I shut the limo door, a breathless Blossom Horowitz, in a low-cut, sequined evening gown, appeared and tapped furiously on the window with a gold-ringed finger. I cracked the glass a bit and couldn't resist saying, "Sorry, all sold out!" as we rolled off into the night.

When we arrived at the Pimlico, we were greeted, as I had hoped, with a royal welcome. Although it was one o'clock in the morning, the place was packed! The owner had leaked rumors about the dinner, and the restaurant had been swamped with reservation requests for the late-night soiree. Cleverly playing his advantage, he showcased our party in full view of the fifty or more gawking guests rather than hide us away in a private room. Liberace embraced the attention and remained as gracious as ever. Ray Arnett, Liberace's stage manager, had told me that Lee's favorite dish was chicken Kiev but that he entrusted its preparation only to a five-star restaurant chef in Beverly Hills. I had never heard of chicken Kiev, but I begged the Pimlico chef to find the best possible recipe. He didn't fail. Liberace was thrilled when the maître d' offered the dish as a special, and when he tasted it, his eyes rolled back in ecstasy and he said, "I want a photograph of this chicken Kiev to put on the mantelpiece beside Mamma!"

He flashed his pearly whites at me, added a wink, and I felt the gods of showbiz smiling down on me.

## Crisis and Kismet

The blue-haired ladies and their blue-collar husbands continued to fill the venue's seats for the rest of the run, and the post-concert repasts were satisfying. Everything was running smoothly until the night when the August heat and humidity skyrocketed, sending the temperature in the tent to an oppressive one-hundred degrees. After the show, Lee uncharacteristically didn't give encores or stay to sign autographs. Suffering from heat exhaustion, he retreated to his air-conditioned hotel room and collapsed. I knew that he couldn't go through another torture session in that tent and that I had to come up with a solution fast to avert disaster. I explained the situation to a young techie on the stage crew who prided himself on being able to fabricate all manner of theatrical gizmos and props. He was on it like Einstein on an equation.

"Leave it to me!"

I arrived at the theater the next morning to find him under the Baldwin, just completing the installation of a rig of six small fans that were directing a flow of air to the seat of the piano stool. "Sit on the stool!" he commanded, smiling broadly. Sure enough, the fans produced a forceful current of air just where I was sitting. "Now look at this," he said, pointing to a black oblong box on top of the piano. The front of the box was open and housed four more small fans. He flipped a toggle switch behind the box, and the fans blew air directly where the pianist would be seated. Then he led me up the ramp to the changing booth to show me where he had installed a large battery-operated fan that cooled the booth perfectly. He had been up all night with his tech buddies procuring parts and rigging fans. I was elated with the results and couldn't wait to show Liberace.

Just as I'd anticipated, Lee and Ray Arnett made an unannounced visit to my office later that day to protest conditions in the tent. Lee described the ordeal of his last performance with exasperation—"It's like going from peacock to baked pheasant, and that's not a dish on my menu!" They threatened to cancel the remaining shows if I couldn't rectify the situation to their satisfaction. I crossed my fingers and offered to give them a demonstration of the improvised cooling system. We went into the tent, and Lee sat down at the piano. A cool breeze blew over him, streaming through his sculptured pompadour and blowing away the suffocating Baltimore heat. He played a few tentative bars and sighed, as his fingers danced in resurgent delight over the ivories. "Reminds me of being in Vegas and going from the street into the lounge—without the cocktails or cabana boys, of course!" he said. "All right, we'll give it a try!"

Whew, a stay of execution!

That night, the show went off without a hitch, improved by the inventive cooling system. No one brought up the subject of the heat again. After the last show, I found out that keeping Lee cool not only saved his sanity and the performances but also contributed to my getting my next job.

Lee's agent, Roger Vorce, and Lee's manager, Seymour Heller, had driven down from New York for the closing show Sunday evening to see their client. I later learned that Lee had spoken to them about my abilities and promising potential. As a result, I was invited to interview at the Agency for the Performing Arts in New York.

## Unbuttoned in Baltimore

Although Liberace flaunted his sexuality and was a flamer, he never acknowledged being gay publicly and successfully sued the press when they reported that he was. Nevertheless, the fact that he was gay was an open secret. This paradox was a result of the sexual taboos surrounding homosexuality at the time.

Working in the arts, I had learned that sexual prejudice didn't exist in the theater community. The actors, singers, and dancers in each touring company lived, worked, and traveled together for the entire summer. To say that these tightly knit families were sexually liberated is an understatement. The revolution that was soon to manifest itself in the era of sex, drugs, and rock 'n' roll was already a fait accompli in these troupes. This exciting world of theater opened my mind and heart to a new sense of freedom and tolerance.

## What Was He Really Like?

Liberace passed away on February 4, 1987, a few months before his sixty-eighth birthday, succumbing to complications from AIDS. Over the years, much has been written about him—the controversy over the hypocrisy of his flamboyantly gay lifestyle and the public image he maintained for fans, his showmanship over musical substance, and the marketing of his offbeat personality. He was recently the subject of an HBO movie starring Michael Douglas and Matt Damon, which brought many questions to light again. Was he a bizarre cultural anomaly? A celebrity fraud? Or just a unique showbiz personality? I couldn't begin to answer those questions nor presume to try. I will say, however, that the man I met in the summer of 1966 was a gracious, polite, and colorful professional whose generosity jump-started my career. To quote Blossom Horowitz: "Lee, you were fabulous!"

# CHAPTER 2

## OFF AND RUNNING

Legs wobbly and head spinning, I stumbled out of the Manhattan offices of the Agency for the Performing Arts (APA) and stopped to collect myself. I had accepted a job as a full-fledged music agent, dealing with world-class talent. Thank you very much, Lee!

It was September 1966. The upheaval of the 1960s had become full eruptions, and with great change comes great opportunity. Based solely on Liberace's recommendation, APA was giving me the chance of a lifetime. The agency was relatively small, yet it had offices across the country and represented some major showbiz figures such as Harry Belafonte, Rowan and Martin, Anita Bryant, and of course, Liberace.

Despite the continued popularity of these classic stars, the company's executives recognized that "the times they are a-changin'." The once-marginalized rock faction in the music industry was on its way to becoming the industry's number-one cash cow. The APA needed someone who was young, hungry, and hip to develop a more popular and profitable line of talent. I was young and certainly hungry, but the hip part—especially New York hip—was dubious.

My job was to identify emerging musical talent who would appeal to college students and be affordable for school programs. That faction had not been lucrative but had promising, untapped potential. I needed to infiltrate the mysterious borderland where the stars of tomorrow were laboring in the obscurity of the present day and then align them with APA. It was a challenge for a twenty-three-year-old newcomer, and I wondered how I was going to make it happen.

## With a Little Help from My Friends

As I went about making my day-to-day contacts with college booking agents and doing my night-to-night talent searches in the New York club world, I made two invaluable contacts: Howie Klein and Steve Paul.

Howie was a student at the State University of New York at Stony Brook. He booked bands for the school and was obsessively plugged into the underground rock scene. He loved nothing more than to talk about what was happening with new music, especially on the West Coast, where bands were making waves that were being felt across the country. A great source of information, with an infectious enthusiasm, Howie was a true believer in the Church of Rock and a constant reminder that we were living in a pivotal time in American history. He kept me informed about what was going on nationally, but I also needed someone locally who could help me actually contact and sign performers.

In 1964, Steve Paul had opened The Scene, on West Forty-Sixth Street, as a laid-back hangout for a Broadway crowd of actors, musicians, and theater people. He was a young guy tuned into the changes in the city's nightlife, which by his definition had gone from showbiz to rock 'n' roll, converting The Scene into a high-energy music club by 1966. Steve and I connected immediately, and his uncanny ability to spot new rock talent and his knowledge of New

York nightspots were invaluable resources. He clued me in to who was hot and where the action was. Pretty soon, I was popping into The Bitter End, Café Au Go-Go, Gerdes Folk City, and Ondine, getting to know the club owners and music business insiders.

## The Agency

It didn't take me long to adjust to working at APA, where everyday life could shift rapidly from the mundane to the memorable. I would typically arrive around midmorning; no one else in the industry was awake or available before then.

One morning, Harvey Litwin, the office manager, was perched on the edge of the desk of our newest and prettiest secretary, Sue. I had heard Harvey's celebrity stories before and was not impressed, but Sue was soaking up Harvey's spiel. "So," he continued, "I said, 'Harry, your timing was perfect; you had the audience in the palm of your hand all night!' And it was true, but you know how they love to hear it! Well, of course, Belafonte comped me a couple of tickets, front table!"

"Wow, Harvey, that's great!" Sue exclaimed.

"Hey, Harvey," I called. "The men's room needs toilet paper. What if Harry Belafonte came in and had to use the john and there was no toilet paper!"

Harvey rolled his eyes and stood up, "Yeah. Okay, wiseguy, I'll take care of it." Actually, I liked Harvey, name-dropping skirt-chaser that he was. Every office needs a joker, and at times, I enjoyed playing that role.

I tried to sneak by the open portal of the office several doors down the hall from mine, but just as I was almost safe I heard Mike Barker shout, "Hey Richard! Come here!"

"Hey, Mike, I was just going to make a call to . . ."

"Aw, c'mon, you gotta see this!" Mike was a short, heavy-set, fast-talking agent who booked novelty acts for the agency. Talking birds, dancing poodles, contortionists—you name it—Mike would book them. The Spanish ventriloquist Señor Wences of "S'okay? S'alright" fame was a big client of his. Military bases were one of his main accounts, and he was always on the lookout for sexy females to entertain the troops.

Mike's enthusiasm drew me in, and even though I'd grown weary of his sideshow clients, I walked over to his magazine- and photo-littered desk. "Check this act out!" he said, handing me a photo of Chinese jugglers tossing deadly looking scimitars back and forth across a stage. "Sullivan is gonna love these guys!" Mike regularly booked his specialty acts on variety shows such as Ed Sullivan's, which was the most popular TV show in America at the time.

"That's cool, Mike!" I said, laying the photo down on top of one of a Rin Tin Tin look-alike jumping through a burning hoop. "Audiences can't get enough of those jugglers, but I really gotta go!"

"Ya wanna see some boobs? I found this chick . . . the GIs are gonna love her." He extended a photo of a voluptuous woman.

"What does she do?"

"Do? I think she sings, maybe dances."

"Wow!" I said, appraising his latest discovery. "I don't think she dances. I don't see how she even walks."

"Sings, dances, who cares? This dame is stacked!"

I loved Mike. He was a living link to the entertainment industry's early vaudeville and burlesque days and a valuable asset to APA, but how many times can you watch Nina, the "Viper Queen," wrap a python around her body?

Back in the hall, I passed Bruce Savan. Bruce was a short, gay man who loved the old-school singers and never missed a chance to dis the rockers. His favorite client was the pop singer John Davidson, whom he had discovered.

"So, Richard, how's the hotshot doing?"

"The hotshot is good, Bruce. How's John Davidson? I heard you got him a month of Sunday afternoon concerts at a Long Island home for old folks."

"Ha ha. Very funny, but let me tell you, mister rock 'n' roll, John will be earning APA money long after your long-haired drug addicts and one-hit wonders are gone!" Bruce pranced quickly down the hall so he didn't have to endure my laughter. We kidded each other mercilessly, but we had one rule: Never hold a grudge.

I had almost made it to my office when the door to the agency's president and founder, David Baumgarten, opened, and out stepped a tall, distinguished-looking man whom I instantly recognized as Harry Belafonte! He smiled. What should I say? I love calypso music? I decided to just smile back as we passed in the hall. I was impressed and couldn't wait to tell Sue about my new friend Harry.

That was agency life—characters, competition, and changes. But even with the constant pressure to find, sign, and book talent, we all got along and cherished our roles as a privileged crew who mingled with stars and had backstage passes to all the action.

## From Blues to the Big Time

While I was learning the ropes at APA, I enjoyed some initial success by bringing in a then-unknown singer-songwriter, Tim Buckley. I had seen Tim perform at the Nite Owl Café on West Third Street in

December 1966 and was impressed by his vocal range and soulful, original songs.

I negotiated a deal with his manager, Herb Cohen, who later became a valuable business friend. APA's bookings helped Tim gain exposure and aided his career, but he was a sensitive soul with a vulnerability that did not fit well with the rigors of the music business; he was a frail flower, struggling to break through a weed patch. I lost contact with him soon after his powerful performance at the Fillmore East in October 1968. When I learned of his accidental death in 1975 at twenty-eight, I was touched and deeply saddened. He continues to be missed by those who adored his unique voice, musical talent, and presence.

Despite my appreciation for the work of so many exciting new artists and my increasing knowledge of the music industry, I was having a soul-searching struggle over whether or not I had made the correct career choice. Self-doubts and lingering anxiety over my ability to achieve meaningful success in such a competitive and often ruthless industry dogged my days. My work at the agency had immersed me in rock, but I was in the blues. Then, one fateful day in January 1967, I got a call from Howie Klein. "Jefferson Airplane is coming to New York!" I couldn't believe it.

"Yeah, I booked 'em to play at Stony Brook," Howie told me. "Keep it quiet for now, but they're also going to be doing a two-week gig at the Au Go-Go."

Howie's tip fired my interest. Jefferson Airplane was the mothership of San Francisco's rock rebellion, flying on the cutting edge of a new sound that was taking over where the British invasion left off. They were communicating directly with the counterculture —the youth culture, the disaffected, and the idealists—who believed that a better day was coming. Their songs were powerful and persuasive, and I wanted to somehow plug into this emerging musical force.

Thanks to Howie, getting a choice seat for the Stony Brook show in February was no problem. But I had to use my APA connection to finagle a ticket to an invitation-only show in January—at RCA's showcase studio Webster Hall—promoting the Airplane's forthcoming album, *Surrealistic Pillow,* which was to become one of the era's landmark albums.

The show at Webster Hall didn't disappoint the packed crowd. The band's signature light show, brought in from San Francisco by their manager, Bill Graham, enhanced the Airplane's performance. Hearing such classics as "White Rabbit" and "Somebody to Love" live for the first time, framed by the novelty of psychedelic illumination, ignited my passion and verified my belief that something new and powerful was happening musically. The show that night blew the roof off the place, and when members of the Paul Butterfield Blues Band, including guitarist Mike Bloomfield, joined the band for its finale, the audience went wild. What a show! What a night. What an inspiration for a young guy eager to be part of the transformation sweeping his generation.

During the Airplane's two-week gig at Café Au Go-Go, I used my industry connections to get backstage and gradually ingratiated myself with Graham. I patiently listened to his psychedelic-poster-hawking schemes and other commercial endeavors, which seemed to be at the forefront of his managerial priorities. To be honest, Bill could be harsh and avaricious, but he was also an innovative promoter and knew how to get things done. I would have a great deal of contact with him in the future, and although we were to have some major differences, he won my professional respect, if not my personal affection.

After a few nights of chumming around with Bill, I invited him to APA's offices to meet my suave and savvy boss, David Baumgarten. The two hit if off like scotch and rocks, and after a few of those, a verbal agreement was reached giving APA exclusive booking rights for Jefferson Airplane outside San Francisco. Representing the premier West Coast rock band gave me a new confidence, and my blues dissolved into the dormouse's refrain— "Feed your head. Feed your head."

In March, "Somebody to Love" was released as a single that scorched the charts. *Look* magazine featured the band in a six-page spread. Jefferson Airplane became synonymous with the Summer of Love, and my phone started ringing off the hook with calls from promoters, agents, and managers of new bands wanting representation. Suddenly, I was a player in the rock 'n' roll business world.

## The Accidental Smuggler

"Don't worry man, they'll just wave you through," Paul Kantner, the Airplane's singer-guitarist, assured me. "The customs cops are all over us, but the way you look, they won't bother you," drummer Spencer Dryden said as he handed me a bag containing a quart jar of fine, manicured marijuana.

"The way you look"? Exactly how did I look? It was a reminder that I was tolerated but not yet accepted into the inner circle. To most people, I appeared to be an ordinary young man, casually dressed in a sport coat and jeans with fashionably—but not rebelliously—long hair. To the members of Jefferson Airplane, gathered in their dressing room after their concert in Toronto's illustrious O'Keefe Center, I looked like a representative of the straight world. The truth was, in the summer of 1967, my feet were planted in both camps—that of the businessman and that of the artist—creating some uncomfortable situations.

I had flown from New York to Toronto to attend Bill Graham's "Sounds of San Francisco," a four-concert series featuring Jefferson Airplane and the Grateful Dead. I wanted to get better acquainted with the Airplane and to schmooze more with Bill. He had just left the dressing room after berating the band for their blasé attitude toward the crowd, which was typical of their insular social outlook. They were a tight-knit group who loved and fought with each other but kept it all inside their own little clique.

After Bill's departure, Spencer motioned me over and asked me if I would do him a favor. He and Grace Slick were not flying back to San Francisco with the rest of the band, but instead going to New York for a romantic getaway. I was thinking maybe he wanted something along the lines of a restaurant recommendation or tips on the local clubs, so I said, "Sure."

What he was actually asking me, in front of the rest of the band, was to smuggle pot across the border—a favor that could have severe legal consequences. I felt the eyes of the band on me. Was this a test? An initiation rite? I could do the sensible thing and beg off, or I could do the reckless, crazy thing.

At customs in Toronto, I tried my best to look cool and relaxed while playing my double-agent role as business executive and rock 'n' roll rebel, but on the inside I was sweating bullets. I guess my conventional, sensible guy disguise was convincing because I sailed through customs and made it back to New York, where I delivered the goods to Spencer. He rewarded his reckless, crazy agent with a tasty baggie of premium pot.

## The Sanctum Sanctorum

With time and a lot of road trips, I got to know the members of the Airplane better. Marty Balin and I became lifelong friends, and Bill Thompson—the band's road manager and eventual full-time manager—became a trusted confidante. It was Bill who introduced me to the pleasures of the high-grade marijuana to which I became a devoted connoisseur.

By the end of 1967, I felt accepted by the band and was confident in my status, demonstrated by the fact that I was a regular member of the after-concert ritual, traditionally conducted in the hotel room of the band's equipment manager. At the hotel after a performance, a secret knock would provide access to the ceremonial room, where a rolled-up towel was wedged beneath the door to keep the strong, sweet scent from wafting down the hall. The "Keeper of the Stash" would break out the sacramental weed to perform the cleansing rite of separating the seeds from the buds. Then came the holy rolling, the lighting of the blessed doobie, and the passing of the mystic weed accompanied by the chant, "Hey man, don't bogart that joint!"

It was a proscribed event performed in a secret manner, with great mirth and affection. The first time I experienced this post-concert ceremony, I thought, "Oh my God, we're gonna get busted." But after a while I just relaxed, got high, and enjoyed the party. Like all true rituals, this celebratory gathering enhanced a sense of community and helped bond us through the years.

## The Doors Come Knocking

Reputations, good and bad, spread quickly through the gossipy entertainment world. During the heady days of March 1967, I got a call from Jac Holzman, the president and founder of Elektra Records. He had heard about APA through Bill Graham and suggested that I check out a new group he'd just signed, The Doors.

The band was still under the radar, but Jac was convinced of their potential and concerned about their managers, a couple of businessmen without industry experience. The band was in New York for a run at Ondine, the trendy club frequented by scene insiders, and Jac invited me to check out the action. I went home that night, smoked a big joint to get into the appropriate mood, and played an advance copy of The Doors' debut album. It blew me away. The arrangements and lyrics worked in harmony to create an album that was poetic and powerful, yet sparse and clean. I couldn't wait to see them in person.

Even in the glamorous and exciting world of show business, some nights are exceptional and create an indelible memory. Although many events get overhyped and don't live up to expectations, The Doors' performance at Ondine was preceded by just the right amount of underground buzz. Ondine was the typical New York nightclub, dark and smoky, with low ceilings and clusters of small tables. Andy Warhol—in his signature black suit, white shirt, and black tie—was surrounded by his flamboyant "Factory" entourage, reporters from the leadings news and entertainment journals poised to record a story, and a swirl of mini-skirted and bell-bottomed entertainment movers and shakers sipping their champagne and cocktails. The atmosphere was charged with curiosity and anticipation.

The band took the stage, and there was Jim Morrison, beautiful and mysterious, skulking around the platform while his band mates struck up "Back Door Man." Before the crowd could catch its breath, it was hearing "Break on Through" and then "Light My Fire." Everyone knew something special was happening. When the band climaxed the show with "The End," you knew what the papers and magazines would be screaming the next day and for days to come. That night, I was more an observer in the club than a member of the "in" crowd, but the important thing was I was there. And I was paying attention. I knew that The Doors were headed for stardom, so I immediately contacted all the necessary parties on the West Coast and in our agency. Before long, I was booking The Doors and helping guide them on their meteoric rise.

## Riders on the Storm

To my dismay, I discovered that shooting stars do not necessarily follow the carefully prescribed courses set out by well-intentioned agents. I began to glimpse the truth of my discovery one night at an after-concert party for The Doors in Rochester, New York.

The concert had gone well, and some fans were hosting an impromptu post-party for the band at a private residence. I was in the living room mingling with friends and fans when I heard a strange barking coming from the kitchen. I investigated and found an inebriated Jim yelping, growling, howling, and laughing under the kitchen table. He was bored, and I guess he had decided to lighten things up a bit. It was time to get him home. I managed to get him back to the hotel, where he stumbled into his room, wobbled toward the desk, pissed in the wastebasket, turned around, and fell on top of the bed. "Jim, are you okay?" He was already snoring loudly as I closed the door behind me.

The next morning, I went down to the restaurant and there was Jim, demonstrating great recuperative powers by wolfing down a huge breakfast, happily socializing with the other band members, and showing no apparent need for the proverbial hair of the dog.

I quickly learned that unpredictability was not limited to human behavior. A massive snowstorm hit Rochester, causing the cancellation of our flight to Boston, where the band was scheduled to play an afternoon and evening show. Scrambling for transportation, we located a local pilot who was willing to fly us in a twin-engine plane to a private Boston airport. I felt the ghosts of Buddy Holly and Richie Valens hovering round as I looked at the old prop job sitting on the snowy runway. Nobody was laughing as we climbed the rickety stairs and took our seats. Bouncing and vibrating, the plane started down the tarmac, slowly, slowly, slowly building momentum until it finally took off and painfully climbed to a cruising altitude. No cocktail-serving stewardesses were onboard to assuage our fears during the bumpy, scary, two-hour flight. When we finally touched down, a chorus of cheers spontaneously erupted. We were two hours late, but the adoring Boston fans got two great performances from a band grateful to be alive.

Drunken rock stars, the vicissitudes of weather, and shady promoters were as much a part of the music biz as creative gratification, the glamour of indulgence, and the seductions of success. The future beckoned with infinite promise, and I was eager to take on all the challenges that it held.

## CHAPTER 3

# MAMMAS DON'T LET YOUR BABIES GROW UP TO BE AGENTS

It is often the case in life that the more enjoyable the benefits of an enterprise, the more noxious the disadvantages. This karmic balance was especially evident in the music industry of the 60s.

I was in my mid-twenties, and having the privilege of working with talented creative contemporaries. We shared much in common: sociopolitical views in a changing world, a love of music, and an ever-increasing appreciation of good weed. Commensurate with these were the often unpleasant and sometimes downright execrable duties of being an agent. My joy at being part of a creative process was juxtaposed with the everyday realities of the business world, creating a tension that would become a determining force during my career.

Those outside the business often think that being an agent means hanging out with the glitterati in plush lounges and reaping substantial percentages of big-money contracts. However, for a guy like me, working his way up, the reality involved representing my clients to ruthless promoters who often had to be tackled on their way to the parking lot to extricate the artist's hard-earned revenues. Getting the artists their fair share of proceeds was neither easy nor enjoyable, but I felt good about protecting their interests and helping them realize their just financial rewards.

Later in my career, when I became a manager, I was able to understand the process of promotion, revenue flow, and fiscal responsibility from another perspective. Agents and managers have distinct duties but work in tandem for artists, creating a system of reciprocal favors. Herb Cohen, who was guiding the careers of Tim Buckley, Linda Ronstadt, and Frank Zappa, was a manager who mentored me in this tradition. In March 1968, as a favor to Herb, I contracted a then unknown Linda Ronstadt and the Stone Ponies to open a weekend of shows for The Doors. When Herb and I arrived at the Colgate College venue, we discovered that it was much larger than I had been told; I had based my fee on the hall's capacity, which meant I had grossly underestimated the take. Herb whipped out two hand counters, which he had learned to carry for just such situations. After informing the promoter, we hand-counted the crowd at the front door, and ended up with a substantially increased earning. Agents and managers were constantly confronted with this type of issue. Even harder to deal with were the naïve and sheltered artists who trusted and listened to uninformed advisors as well as the eccentric and egotistical personalities whose sudden rise to fame had inflated their sense of self-importance and made them impossible to work with.

## The Electric Circus

The serrated flashes of the strobe, the absurdist images swirling across every wall, the flame-throwing jugglers, and the creepy clowns set the tone for the Electric Circus—a cavernous discotheque that represented the wild aspect of the New York city club scene in 1967. David Rubinson, a Columbia record producer, tipped me off that this matrix of uptown chic and downtown hip was the place to catch the up-and-coming Chambers Brothers.

The Chambers Brothers were four real-life brothers who'd grown up in rural Mississippi and moved to Los Angeles. They electrified their gospel-blues music, causing a sensation at the Newport Folk Festival. Their eclectic style produced a hit single, "Time Has Come Today," and they were beginning to establish themselves as a favorite with a range of audiences. They defied categorization. I had no idea what to expect from them, but what I saw and heard immediately made me a fan. Audiences embraced their engaging style, and their love of performing was obvious.

They were guitar based, but their vocal harmonies were the heart of their appeal. They added a drummer to drive their gospel-rock and Motown fusion, enhancing their rhythmic arrangements. Even the Fellini-esque atmosphere of the Electric Circus could not detract from their soulful covers of "People Get Ready" and "Midnight Hour," as attested by the audience's ecstatic ovations. Backstage, I introduced myself and told them how much I loved their music. They were genuine and down-to-earth, and we quickly established an easy rapport.

I was excited by their potential and offered to work on their behalf; we set up a meeting with their manager, a record company accountant happy to turn over the reins of their career to someone who was actually enthused about promoting them. I liked the Chambers brothers as people, and I believed in their music. They had a familial cohesiveness that was nurtured early in life, when they sang together in their Mississippi Baptist church choir. This affinity spurred me to work hard to help them achieve success. I got them on as the opening act for The Doors and procured engagements from Massachusetts to Florida. Consequently, their income and industry recognition increased significantly. We got along well and it was a pleasure working with them—until the sugar turned to shit.

Our easy, friendly relationship disintegrated the day the brothers arrived in my office with an "official" manager. One look at the man and I saw trouble. He was jive-ass and clearly in it for a quick killing. Artists are vulnerable to praise, especially when they are on their way up, and it's often difficult for them to make the right choices. I had no idea how they'd found this guy; he was all the Chambers brothers weren't: an angry black dude dressed in a shiny black suit and sporting a cane, a derby, and a mean-spirited countenance.

He didn't look into my eyes when Lester Chambers introduced him to me, and not once during the entire meeting did he ever convey a cooperative spirit or friendly attitude toward me. Instead, I got, "Listen here, young white boy, you may have been calling the shots with the brothers, but now things are going to change!" He wasted no time getting to the point of his visit. "Now that I'm here, I want to see some *real* money coming in. The brothers are underpaid, and I want to know why they aren't getting as large a concert guarantee from promoters as The Doors." The tension in the room was as thick as his contempt for me, but I presented my most reassuring smile, thinking that if I offered a calm, rational explanation, he'd cool down. He didn't.

"Well," I said, "The brothers have only had one hit single. One song isn't the only factor that determines live performance earnings. It takes time to develop a following." He didn't seem to be picking up on what I was putting down, so I decided to be more direct. "Jim is a sex symbol. He attracts thousands of teenyboppers. He's been on national television and the focus of media attention. I love the

Chambers Brothers and the agency is doing all it can to further their career."

The sneer never left his face. He didn't want to hear anything I was saying. His agenda for the meeting was to berate me and inflate his own importance to the group. He criticized the job we were doing to validate his position as a ball-breaking manager who was going to shake things up. The brothers knew I had been working hard for them and were clearly embarrassed. I looked over at Lester, whose downturned eyes revealed the shame he felt.

After that meeting, I was no longer allowed to have a one-on-one relationship with any of the brothers. I never saw them again without the presence of their manager. He interfered at every turn and destroyed the personal relationship that the agency and I had with the guys. We continued to get them higher paying gigs and placed them on bills with The Doors, Jefferson Airplane, Jimi Hendrix, and other groups of prominence we represented, but the camaraderie between artist and rep was lost. Why the brothers followed this guy I'll never know. Maybe the reason had something to do with race, because during this time African Americans were asserting themselves and viewing the white establishment with suspicion and mistrust. Whatever the reason, it was an unfortunate example of how artist-manager relationships can wreak havoc for an agent.

# CHAPTER 4

# BAD BOYS AND REALLY BIG SHEWS

Chicks dig bad boys, and the baddest boy in New York City in August 1967 was Jim Morrison.

Elektra Records was throwing a party in celebration of The Doors' success, and Danny Fields, Elektra's publicist, invited me to go. I finished up a few things that I had to do at my desk and got ready to walk over to Park Avenue. I copped a nickel bag of weed from Sammy, our office boy, and went to the restroom to perform what had become for me a common ritual: I rolled a joint, lit it while standing on the hopper, and blew the smoke out the ceiling exhaust fan. In a few minutes, I was out the door, good to go. As I walked, I began to reflect on recent events in my life. Less than a year ago, I was in Baltimore, fresh out of college, naïve, and working with Liberace. And now I was in New York, getting high, traveling, and working with rock stars.

I remembered having heard that in August 1964, three years earlier, Bob Dylan had come down from Woodstock to the same Delmonico Hotel where I was headed, to turn on The Beatles to marijuana. The times they were a-changin' indeed.

Dylan had taken LSD in the spring of 1964, an experience that transformed his music. He was not the only one experimenting, and the fusion of rock and psychedelics was affecting our culture dramatically and transforming the way some of us looked at the world. In just three years, rock music had gone from "I Wanna Hold Your Hand" to John Lennon's Timothy Leary-inspired "Tomorrow Never Knows."

I arrived at the Delmonico, higher than I wanted to be. After all, I was the business guy and should have been maintaining a modicum of sobriety. I was directed to the wine cellar, where the party was well under way. The Doors' New York friends, along with the usual crowd of industry functionaries, hangers-on, reporters, beautiful people, and pseudo-beautiful people who suck up to the stars, were on hand to guzzle free booze. Jim was at the center of it all, his handsome face framed by cascading ringlets of dark hair, dressed in a black leather suit, white shirt, and skinny black tie and posing for publicity shots. "Light My Fire" was the number-one single in the country for the third week in a row, and this was truly Jim's moment in time. Andy Warhol and his campy Factory crew were fawning over him, and men and women with various sexual preferences ogled him as they sipped their favorite drinks. The scene looked like a Renaissance painting of some lost angel surrounded by nymphs and satyrs—an ode to the elegance of corruption.

Sitting at a nearby table, I watched, more than a little starstruck, as Andy presented Jim with an ornate antique French plastic phone with a rotary dial. Jim laughed out loud—it was a preposterous gift. "Thanks, Andy. That's just what I wanted!" he said, without intending to insult him because the phone was obviously a campy gift. I could see that Andy was taken with Jim, which was no surprise because Jim was happening, handsome, unabashedly sexy, and charismatic. Andy was a gay artist, a powerful player in the New York scene who usually got whatever he desired. I could overhear Andy's overtures to Jim, insisting that he visit The Factory.

"I'd love to film you, Jim!" Andy entreated while his choir of minions cooed in assent, but Jim was having none of it. The drunker he got, the more he began to toy with Warhol and put him on. All attention was riveted on the two stars, but Jim tired of it quickly and shifted his focus to the feast before him. At this point, the gathering was becoming more of a Doors celebration, with local friends and insiders and fewer industry people. Everybody was loosening up, and Jim was pulling out vintage bottles of wine from the racks and passing them around. As he emptied his glass of fine French wine, he called out, "We're hungry! More food!" Doors music played loudly, and Jim began throwing ice cubes at the many groupies, which drew boisterous laughter from the crowd. People were lighting up joints, and the smell of weed pervaded the room.

All the publicity shots had been taken, and the music executives, the press, and those not committed to continuing the Dionysian ritual of overindulgence departed, leaving the hard-core partyers and curious bystanders like myself. The affair finally concluded when the Delmonico's banquet manager arrived to find Jim lurching precariously on top of a table, knocking over wine glasses and smashing canapés. The manager's indignant shouts signaled that the real world was about to intrude on the Bacchanalian fantasy. Within minutes, the police were on the scene and emptying the room. The band and their friends—giddy and booze- and dope-infused—stumbled onto Park Avenue and into their awaiting limousines. I looked on incredulously and chuckled to myself, remembering that just a couple of hours ago I was thinking I might be too high for the event. The evening was young for the departed revelers, but I threaded my way home through the streets of New York, amused by the recollections of the evening and unaware that I would play a greater role in the Morrison drama.

## Ed, We Couldn't Get Much Higher or Care Less

A month or so after the Delmonico party, in September 1967, The Doors were still atop the charts with their number-one single "Light My Fire" and were scheduled to make a live appearance on the *Ed Sullivan Show.*

It is hard to overstate the power that this singular television show exerted on national taste. The show itself was like a throwback to vaudeville, with a mix of circus acts, musical talent, and skits. Its host—Ed Sullivan—was neither an entertainer nor a vivacious personality. In fact, he was a bland, nondescript little man—parodied by Americans across the country for his signature phrase— "really big *shew.*" Ed, though, had introduced Elvis, The Beatles, and the Rolling Stones to America, and an appearance on his show represented the pinnacle of success and exposure. The deeply conservative Ed and the CBS brass had shown Elvis from the waist up, not allowing his pelvic gyrations to be seen, and had convinced the Stones to change their lyrics from "let's spend the night together" to "let's spend some time together." I knew the meeting of the brash, unapologetic Doors and the uber-straight Ed would make for an interesting encounter, so I used my agency connection to be on hand backstage.

A considerable amount of pre-performance tension existed between The Doors and the show's staff. Ed tried to cozy up to the boys after the sound check by saying, "You boys look great when you smile! Do that tonight—you're too serious." It was an odd comment from the guy who was known for never smiling. The band goofed about that for a while and joked among themselves about Ed's awkward and patronizing manner.

While the band was making pre-show preparations, Ed's son-in-law producer, Bob Precht, appeared and informed Jim that he had to find an alternative to the lyric, "higher." Jim gave him the ole "fuck you" response. Ray Manzarek, the band's keyboardist and resident diplomat, interceded between the defiant Jim and the tight-jawed producer and assured Precht that he had nothing to worry about. After Precht left the room, I reminded them that back in 1963, CBS network censors had forbidden Dylan to perform "Talkin' John Birch Paranoid Blues," and with uncompromising integrity, Dylan walked out on the show. Jim said he would have nothing to do with censorship and was not about to change the lyrics for anyone. The group quietly conspired to keep the lyrics intact. As the agency rep, I could have tried to dissuade them, but I was on the side of the artists and free speech and shrugged, "What can they do?"

True to his rebellious nature, Morrison sang the word "higher" not once but twice, touching off wild cheers and applause from the audience. After the show, Precht stormed into the dressing room, furious at the group for breaking their promise. He shouted at Jim, "You'll never do the Sullivan Show again!" For once, Jim was perfectly calm as he concisely summed up the band's response.

"Who cares? We just did it."

As the fall of 1967 turned to winter, it became more and more my professional and personal duty to care for, and about, Jim Morrison.

# Chapter 5

## Bailing Out Baudelaire

Jim Morrison—the beautiful bad boy Baudelaire of rock—prowled the stage of the New Haven Arena. His signature dark curls snaked down over his shoulders, and his tight black leather pants rippled in the spotlight. The audience loved it! The crowd was his. He grew more intense and his eyes flashed anger. He didn't sing—he spoke. In a voice filled with passion, he described an incident that had occurred backstage just before the show; it had ignited his combustible temper, and he was seething. The incident would later prove to be the catalyst for one of the most notorious moments in rock history.

In November 1967, The Doors were experiencing a sudden rise in popularity and their management asked me to book several East Coast concerts during the holiday season. The band had a gold album, and feature articles in *Time, Newsweek,* and *Vogue* presented them as outlaws, a cachet that attracted legions of loyal fans. I had some difficulty finding venues on such short notice, but I managed to book them a show in Troy, New York, at the Rensselaer Polytechnic Institute, and a show in New Haven, Connecticut, at the Arena the following night.

The show in Troy went on as scheduled December 8. It was Jim's birthday, and he wanted the evening concert to be not only a special celebration of his birthday but also a vindication of his art and a salute to the band's success. The band tried its best to connect with the RPI audience with highly energized performances of "Back Door Man" and "Break on Through," but they didn't seem to be able to relate to The Doors' cutting-edge sound or Jim's dark, mystic chants and soul-wrenching screams. At the end of the truncated one-hour show, a frustrated Jim screamed into the mic.

"If this is Troy, I'm with the fuckin' Greeks!"

The RPI kids, apparently great at understanding science, were not great at understanding music. Their response was tepid, and their polite hand clapping was an obvious and huge disappointment to Jim.

It was not the reaction he wanted to the band's passion and fury, especially tonight of all nights—his birthday—when he was striving for a spirit-sharing orgy of sweat-soaked communion.

As the booking agent, I felt somewhat responsible for the audience-performer mismatch, but I was as surprised at the tepid response as Jim was frustrated and disappointed. I had had a spooky premonition about these shows, and the poor reception in Troy was an uncomfortable reminder. I tried not to think about it, and reassured the nonplussed media reps that the New Haven show would make their trek worthwhile.

On the way up to New Haven before the show, Ray Manzarek and I, with our girlfriends, stopped for dinner at a country inn in Connecticut. Jim was scheduled to take a limo from New York and meet us at the venue an hour before the show. The arrangements were clear and simple, but all through dinner and on the rest of the drive to New Haven my conscience, a lousy companion on a rock tour, kept nagging me for letting Jim out of my sight. Ray was having the same apprehensions, and talking to him about it did little to allay my fears. I should have been at the arena keeping a watchful eye over the evening's proceedings, and stopping for dinner was feeling more and more like a risky indulgence.

The New Haven venue—a typical nondescript downtown sports arena—had been pressed into service quickly for the concert, and the large police presence on the street outside attested to the city's paranoia about hosting an event with superstar subversives. Walking through the Arena's concrete catacombs, I saw cops outing groupies who had attempted to hide in janitorial closets, under concession stand counters, and in whatever spots they thought would secret them in hopes of getting closer to their heroes. As I approached the locker room, the makeshift dressing room for the concert, Jim burst through the door, hands pressed to his eyes, screaming. "I've been Maced! The fuckin' pig Maced me!"

Bill Siddons, the band's young road manager, ran past me, grabbed Jim, and led him inside to a sink, where he helped him flush out his eyes. Within minutes, I was negotiating peace talks with Lieutenant Kelly, the police commander, and the underling who was responsible for spraying the Mace in Jim's face. Jim was a short distance away, trying to wash out the chemicals and raging against fascist brutality. The cop justified what he'd done, parroting: "Just following orders!" with a self-serving emphasis on performing his duty. It was obvious that he hadn't recognized Jim. I could hear Jim in the background, the angry victim, mimicking a refrain in his song: "We want the world and we want it now!"

"I want an apology and I want it NOW!"

I knew Jim would not perform without an apology but I didn't see one coming. I jumped in and played the "possible riot" card. "You have two thousand revved-up fans here! If Jim refuses to play, all hell will break loose!" I screamed in desperation at the lieutenant, hoping he would realize the volatility of the situation. I could see he was thinking it over. Finally, he nodded to his subordinate, who looked over at the red-eyed, righteously indignant victim of authoritarian oppression.

"Sorry. No hard feelings, eh, Jim?"

"That's it?" Jim said.

The cops shrugged and ambled off, thinking all was resolved. I, however, had seen the look in Jim's sore, swollen eyes as the smug excuse for an apology was being delivered and knew that the affair was far from over. I feared that he, the guiltless victim of police brutality, would in some way have his own wild justice.

When he finally took the stage, the news of his having been Maced had already burned through the crowd and he was greeted like a war hero. It was now us versus the cops, and the cops were strategically positioned around the hall, easy, big, blue targets for the fan's animosity. The revolution in black leather pants never looked sexier striding across the stage, livid with inspired indignation. It was a micro-minute with all the cultural DNA of the era. To quote Dylan: "There was music in the cafés at night and revolution in the air." Tonight, Jim was neither loaded on booze nor hyped on drugs; he was running on high-octane anger and the audience was with him one hundred percent. The band launched into the third song of the set, "Back Door Man," and Jim took advantage of an extended instrumental break to move to the edge of the stage and address the crowd. My inner oracle was jumping up and down on my sinking heart; I knew what was about to hit.

"I want to tell you something that happened just a few minutes ago right here in New Haven . . . this is New Haven, isn't it? New Haven, Connecticut, United States of America?" The shouts of the crowd attested to the fact that it was indeed New Haven and they didn't like that their visiting rock god had been abused in their own hometown. Feeding off the energy of the frenzied audience, Jim launched into his narrative of how he had met this girl from a local college at dinner and invited her to the concert.

"We were in the dressing room, talking . . . and we wanted some privacy, you know. . ."

It was easy for every girl in the audience to fantasize about being that girl with Jim, and they listened with rapt attention.

". . . so we went into the shower room . . . we weren't doin' anything, just standin' there talkin' . . . then this little man came up . . . this little man in a little blue suit and a little blue . . . hat. . ."

The room was hanging on every word.

"An' he said, 'whatcha doin' there?'"

"Nuthin' . . . But he didn't go away. He just stood there, reached behind his back, and brought out this little can of something . . . looked like shaving cream . . . and then . . . he sprayed it in MY EYES! I was BLINDED for about thirty minutes. . . ."

Every girl's fantasy turned into every girl's nightmare, and the young women in the front row started calling the cops guarding the stage "pigs" and "scumbags." Nothing unites a group like a common enemy. The crowd booed loudly and the boys in blue responded by jutting their jaws and tightening their lines. From my vantage point just off stage, I could feel the hostility sweeping through the arena. My premonition of trouble was manifesting on a scale beyond my worst fears. Jim and the crowd were feeding off each other's anger, and as their defiance grew bolder, the police strained at their collective leash, eager to put the bite on their detractors. Power mad and ego wounded, Jim continued to up the ante. He strutted, postured, and then suddenly screamed into the mic!

"WE WANT THE FUCKING WORLD AND WE WANT IT NOW!"

At that moment, as if scripted, the lights came on. Ray, sensing big-time trouble, walked over to Jim and whispered something in his ear. Jim seemed to calm down and asked the crowd if they wanted to hear music. A chorus of "Yes" erupted, but it was too late. The battle had been initiated and had to play itself out. Cops swarmed the stage and Lieutenant Kelly made his entrance from stage left. Jim pointed his mic at him like a blade.

"Say your thing, man!" Whether he was taunting or offering equal time for a rebuttal is a moot point.

"You've gone too far, young man!" Kelly responded with authority.

A cop snatched the mic out of Jim's hand. The battle was over and history was in the making. Jim Morrison became the first rock star to be arrested on stage. As the cops took him away, I stood there terror-stricken, wondering what I should do next. I knew it would be futile to intercede, but I fought my way through the crowd and onto the stage. Amidst the chaos, I reassured Ray that I'd go to the station and see that Jim was bailed out. I suggested that he take one of the limos back to New York with Robby and John, as the police quickly formed a line across the elevated stage, blocking the access of an increasingly irate and raucous crowd. Several cops escorted Jim through a parted curtain at the rear of the stage, down the ramp, and out the back door toward a squad car, where a small crowd had already started to gather. I was following as closely as I could. Jim began to resist and the cops welcomed the opportunity to pounce, knocking him to the ground and delivering several uncalled-for kicks.

"He's not resisting arrest!" I shouted and pleaded with them to stop beating him. The cops thought Jim was an impudent, arrogant punk and would have happily beaten the shit out of him had it not been for the interventions, protests, and pleas of onlookers. Yvonne Chabrier, a *Life* reporter, Tim Page, a *Life* photographer, and Michael Zwerin, a critic for the *Village Voice*, were all arrested for allegedly interfering with Morrison's arrest. They were in fact simply protecting him from a brutal beating.

It was a harrowing moment for me. I was responsible not only for the show but also for Jim's personal safety. The situation was spinning out of control, and I couldn't allow myself to get arrested because someone had to bail out Baudelaire. The cops threw Jim in the squad car and took off. I looked around in a panic, spotted our limo and driver in the reserved parking area, and ran to him for help. The two of us followed in hot pursuit.

The sergeant behind the front desk, more accustomed to cashing out drunks and wife beaters than celebrities, answered my questions with a caution tinged with suspicion. Jim was charged with "breaching the peace," "immoral exhibition," and "resisting arrest." Bail was set at fifteen hundred dollars. Fortunately, I had insisted on being paid in cash before the show and had a couple of grand in concert money in my pocket. I pulled out the wad, laid down the sum before the sergeant's disbelieving eyes, and asked for a receipt. The cop's glare told me he didn't appreciate being patronized by a young New York City hotshot, and he made his point by letting me cool my heels for a small eternity while he disappeared to process Jim's release. Finally, he reappeared with a disheveled, smirking

Morrison, and minutes later we were making our way through a cheering crowd of fans gathered outside the station.

God, was I thankful to be out of that hellhole! I turned to Jim and uttered a deep sigh of relief as we pulled away from the station. Jim was smiling that innocent, sheepish, little smile of his that I had seen many times before at hotel breakfast tables the morning after one of his unruly, post-concert blowouts.

A glorious dawn was breaking as our limo arrived in Manhattan, and in my head I was mulling over whether putting on shows in small towns featuring prima donna superstars was the rewarding career in music I wanted. Jim, who had been napping since his jailhouse adventure, woke up, yawned, and looked out the window at the world beyond.

"I'd like to do a piece of music one day that's a pure expression of joy. Like a celebration of existence . . . like the coming of spring and the sun rising . . . pure, unbounded joy."

It was a poetic turn of phrase I had known him to recite before. That was the other Jim: sweet, sensitive, beguiling, and full of love for life. He put me through the wringer as his agent, but so much about him was joyous. When he connected with his audience, his performance became a ritual that fused music, spectacle, and poetry. He had his demons and embraced excess but remained true to his mad, poetic vision. He was genuine, exciting, talented, and uncompromised. His self-destructive recklessness gave him a vulnerability and charisma that made him irresistible.

Jim dared to challenge himself more than most of us have the courage to do or could even imagine. He followed the rhythms of his own wild spirit, lived his truth to its dangerous fullest, said what he had to say, and left. He never kowtowed to anyone. I secretly relished his impudence in the face of authority. He was acting on behalf of our generation.

He told me once he never liked the idea of getting old, which was prophetic because he died at the age of twenty-seven.

Although deeply saddened by his death, it was as predictable as the fiery end of a shooting star.

"Wild child, full of grace, savior of the human race."

# CHAPTER 6

# OLD MONEY AND NEW MUSIC

Wandering through the posh Georgetown mansion of former New York Governor Averell Harriman and rubbing shoulders with the stars of the Democratic Party had me feeling like a tourist in wonderland, oddly out of place but enjoying the magic. Adding to my great joy, there was not one bar but many to fuel my giddy sense of unreality. As more of the rich and famous arrived, I tippled my way through the gilded chambers.

This unlikely scenario was a result of the strange bedfellows syndrome that occurred in the late 1960s. The establishment—liberal, East Coast, old-money families—began to recognize not only the cultural importance of rock music but its political potential as well. Rock had become the youth anthem and was a force to be reckoned with. Its raw, aggressive sounds and unapologetic voices accompanied the multitudes marching in the streets and also grabbed the good old boys by their starched collars. The unity of this alliance and its exotic mix of elements created some memorable moments.

In February 1968, Ethel Kennedy, the queen mother of progressive Democrats, was sponsoring a telethon for children with mental disabilities at a Washington TV station. A Learjet had been commissioned to fly Jefferson Airplane—the hot new San Francisco group and now my clients—to the event. The connection between the charity fundraiser and the band was their admiration for the antiwar, liberal policies of Robert Kennedy.

The Harrimans had volunteered their mansion as the shuttle base and party pad for celebrities going to and from the television station. Harriman—scion of an old-time robber baron—was a widely respected elder statesman and former diplomat who was not in the habit of opening his private residence to young upstarts in the entertainment industry, but he did so graciously. I was curious to glimpse the lifestyle of American aristocracy, and the prospect of free food and booze while gawking at the privileged and powerful promised to elevate my experience to a working-class fantasy. I saw myself as a socially conscious spy, secretly there on behalf of the everyman class: the dope-smoking class, the bohemian class, and the crass, classless class.

I arrived at the mansion unfashionably early and was ushered into an immense room filled with antique furniture and elaborately framed oil paintings. The trappings of wealth and privilege were overwhelming, and my social-political indignation and ideals were being seriously challenged by the seduction of old-money elegance.

A well-dressed woman in her mid-sixties approached, and I thought she was going to ask to see my invitation. Instead, she said, "Hello, I'm Marie Harriman. Welcome to our home!"

I introduced myself and commented on the exquisite character of her furnishings.

"Well, I was a dealer at one time," she said.

As I amused myself with thoughts of asking if she had a spare doobie, she waved at the paintings and continued.

"But that was when I had the gallery on Fifty-seventh Street. After it closed, we donated most of the important works to the National Gallery. Are you a collector?"

"No, but I'm a pretty good thief."

She laughed. "I love a good bargain, too!"

I motioned to the masterpieces, "Looks like you've hit some pretty high-end flea markets." We shared a laugh and were enjoying each other's company. She nodded to a waiter who brought over a tray of drinks and canapés.

"What line of work are you in?" she asked.

"The music business."

"Oh, do you know the pianist Peter Duchin? Av and I raised him after his mother died. His father was Eddy Duchin, the bandleader. You must know Peter!"

Suddenly, I felt like I was talking to the Mother Teresa of Tiffany's. I could have chitchatted with Marie and sucked down champagne for hours, but the place was starting to fill up and she had bigger fish to charm. Socially, I was just a sardine, but she sweetly patted my little fin, smiled, and tottered off to chat up some newly arrived great whites while I swam off in search of the nearest bathroom to fire up a joint.

Returning to the gathering crowd, I spotted Lauren Bacall just a few feet away with a short guy I made out to be Jason Robards, Jr. She was probably in her mid-forties, stunningly svelte and beautiful in a long black evening gown. She caught my stare and gave me a polite smile. Then I saw Woody Allen sitting cross-legged on the floor doing card tricks, and across from him, my childhood baseball hero, Stan Musial. Stan was mesmerized by Woody's sleight of hand and oblivious to my awe-inspired gaze. I stood there for a while, similarly transfixed by Woody's card mastery. Looking up, I saw the comedy team of Stiller and Meara. As our eyes locked, I tossed a nod of recognition and went on my way, looking for stars of greater prominence, having quickly become selective about whom I would spend my celebrity fantasy time with.

Then I saw him: Bobby Kennedy. I almost lost my newfound cool. I did a double take to make sure it was he.

Nobody was giving him hugs or posing with him for snapshots, but sure enough, it was Bobby Kennedy.

Incredibly, he was alone. I suddenly experienced the sense of some larger force—fate, destiny, or maybe the weed I'd just smoked—intervening and allowing this chance meeting between the people's champion and me, a twenty-five-year-old punk agent.

As I approached, it occurred to me that I didn't know how to address him. He wasn't a senator; he was no longer attorney general. Was he just Mr. Kennedy? That didn't sound right. Neither did, Hey, Bobby! I was tongue-tied. Thankfully, he spoke first, extending his hand. "Robert Kennedy. Pleased to meet you."

As I introduced myself, I noticed a thin, beaded bracelet on his wrist, so incongruous but cool. Underneath the tailored suit and Harvard education, Bobby was a hippie, a peacenik, one of us, a man with whom I could relax and speak my heart. "It's so great to have your voice against the war. You've really given us hope, and it's reassuring to know there are some sane people in Washington," I said, still hardly believing it was he.

"It's been very difficult to get the kind of help we need to end the war, and that's why I'm particularly grateful to the music and entertainment industry, people like yourself, who have been such strong supporters of our efforts," the ever-gracious politician replied.

We went back and forth for a while, congratulating each other and vowing to keep up the good fight. Our conversation came to an end, and as we shook hands I said, "Love the bracelet, by the way."

He looked down at his wrist. "Oh, one of my kids slipped it on this morning. Forgot all about it." He smiled, pulled it off, and stuffed it into his pocket. So much for idols, I thought, and went off looking for more celebs.

My celebrity hobnobbing was interrupted by an announcement that it was time to leave for the TV station.

Bill Thompson, the Airplane's manager, ushered the band members and me into several waiting limos, and we headed to the station to hang out until it was the Airplane's turn to perform. Backstage, I wandered over to Bill, who was talking to a beefy guy with a cigar; Bill turned to me and motioned to his companion, "Richard, this is Pierre Salinger."

Salinger had been JFK's press secretary and was part of the Kennedy inner circle. He was friendly and seemed like an affable guy. At Thompson's suggestion, he had agreed to appear with the band, pretending to accompany Grace on the piano during her performance of "Rejoyce," a song she had written.

The band and Salinger took the stage, and Grace, well oiled with patrician booze, started belting out her lyrics. The song parodied JFK's "Ask not what your country can do for you" with "War is good business so give me your son, but I would rather have my country die for me." As political protest goes, it was subtle. No one seemed to notice, certainly not Pierre, who was having a great time ripping off imaginary riffs. It was a nice moment—a famous politician playing at being a rock star, and famous rock stars playing at politics.

After the show, we returned to the Harriman mansion, where

the party raged on until the band and I stumbled back to our hotel in the wee hours, much impressed with the after-hours stamina of the East Coast elite. We had no idea what life in the big leagues was all about, however, until later that morning, when we were all graciously escorted to a party hosted by the Kennedys at their Hickory Hill compound in Virginia.

I found myself sitting on their enclosed patio, sipping a Mimosa in hopes of easing my massive hangover and holding a plate of scrambled eggs and bacon. I set down my plate for a moment to take in the beauty of the sunshine pouring over the landscaped grounds. When I reached back to retrieve my food, I felt instead a dense mat of fur. Turning, I saw a Newfoundland dog licking the eggs off my plate. I instinctively pulled my Mimosa out of the tongue range of the great beast and heard someone laugh behind me.

"Don't worry, he prefers Bloody Marys," Ted Kennedy said, smiling down at us. I stood up to introduce myself, and he said, "Sorry about Brumus's manners."

"Yeah," I said, watching my bacon disappear into Brumus's slobbering mouth. Ted and I had a relaxed time sipping our Mimosas, trading observations on life and politics, with Brumus close at hand—not wanting to miss a social opportunity or an unguarded plate. Brumus was a party animal with style, charm, and a pedigree, and his picture eventually wound up on the inside sleeve of the Airplane's *Crown of Creation* album.

I never got over my hangover that afternoon, despite my best hair-of-the-dog efforts, but hanging out with the likes of Andy Williams, Perry Como, Tommy Smothers, the Kennedys, and Brumus on that intoxicated, golden day in the Elysian Fields of Kennedyland was worth every throbbing moment.

# Chapter 7

## Doorway to Disaster

"Jim wants to quit the band!"

"What?" I couldn't believe my ears! Todd Shiffman, my colleague on the West Coast, was calling to tell me that Jim Morrison wanted to quit The Doors!

"You're kidding! Why?" I asked.

"Says he's having a nervous breakdown," Todd replied. "He wants the band to get another singer."

"Did you hear that from Jim himself?"

"No. Bill Siddons. Then he called me back a second time to say that Ray was trying to talk Jim out of it, but you might have to cancel the East Coast shows."

"Tell Bill to tell the band we're talkin' about a quarter of a million dollars in lost income, not to mention lawsuits!" I said, forcing my voice to stay calm and firm. It was the summer of 1968, and *Waiting for the Sun,* The Doors' third LP, and "Hello, I Love You," a single from the album, had hit number one on the charts simultaneously. The Doors were the hottest commodity on the music market. When Todd called, I was putting the final touches on their four upcoming East Coast concerts.

Why would Jim want to quit the band? He had never threatened to quit before. The band was tight. With Ray on keyboards, Robby Krieger on guitar, and John Densmore on drums, the music was strong and impeccably arranged to underscore Jim's poetry and stage choreography. The band seemed almost telepathically connected, and I had never witnessed them in musical disputes or at each other's throats in the dressing room after a performance. That was rare in bands. The Doors didn't do lengthy, grueling tours that physically wore them out, and Jim loved the excitement of live theater performance. At heart he was a poet, and this poet had a backup band. I had heard a lot from Todd and Ray about his tempestuous relationship with his on-again-off-again soul mate, Pam Courson. While wondering whether she could be the one making demands, the phone rang. It was Todd.

"Pam demanded that Jim quit the band or she's leaving him. Ray asked him to give it six months and promised to break up the band after that if he still feels the same way. Last word was he agreed. I'll keep you posted," Todd reported and hung up.

I had my answer.

## Weekend in Hell

I had a reprieve, but the incident felt ominous. The first weekend of August 1968, I had booked the band into four consecutive concerts: Bridgeport, Connecticut; Queens, New York; Cleveland, Ohio; and Philadelphia. The band had hired a film crew to shoot a full-length documentary, and the crew would be recording the action constantly, adding an extra element of tension and pressure. As their agent, I had multiple tasks: dealing with promoters, collecting revenues, greeting the band at airports, and making sure they arrived at the venue on time and reasonably sober. The most taxing tasks were having Jim arrive on time for the performance and reasonably sober. I later heard Ray Manzarek in an interview sum up the situation perfectly: "Jim had to live on the edge twenty-four hours a day . . . it was hard to go on the road . . . to get on airplanes and go to airports . . . that stuff was really hard to do."

The first night in Bridgeport was more or less uneventful. An hour prior to the show, at stone-sober Jim's request, I escorted him to a solitary dressing room where he turned off the lights and locked himself away from all distractions. This behavior, which he exhibited every so often, was an interesting meditative contrast to his mercurial moments.

Jim played with his eyes closed through most of the show, hanging on to the microphone as if to steady himself. It was a subdued performance without the fiery antics many fans had come to expect. He was being his unpredictable self, and it made me nervous.

The Singer Bowl concert in Queens the next day was the biggest outdoor concert of the year for The Doors, and The Who was opening. The hot and humid weather intensified the much-anticipated meeting of the two bands. The Who had not yet achieved rock icon status, but they were ready to impress the crowd with their high-energy music and theatrics. An air of energized, unspoken rivalry between the bands created an almost palpable tension that was fueling the raucous New York audience.

The opening set was vintage Who. Townshend wind-milled his arms, Daltry twirled his microphone with precision, and the music was LOUD!

They ended their piss-and-vinegar portion of the concert with "My Generation" and the customary smashing of their instruments.

Technical problems, one involving a major malfunction with the revolving stage, created a frustrating one-hour delay between acts, and you could feel the crowd's edginess and impatience growing.

The Doors finally took the stage, and NYPD's finest formed a line on the stage between the band and the audience and began to repel the onrush of frenzied fans. To make matters worse, the motorized stage ceased to rotate without warning, allowing fans to rush the stage and escalating the confrontation. Jim, always intrigued by violence and mob mentality, immediately connected to the crowd and started playing with their energy. He accelerated his wild improvised dancing, amplified his carnal shrieks, and reached out to the hands trying to grab him as the police tried to intervene and keep it all from happening.

Pete Townshend was standing next to me offstage witnessing the unruly scene. He expressed amazement at how Morrison was purposely calculating and intensifying the crowd's moods, taking them from adulation to rapture to chaos and violence. "Are riots commonplace at Doors concerts?" he asked as the events on the stage continued to spin out of control.

"They're exaggerated by the media for the sensational aspect," I said. "But Jim is unpredictable. It's part of his power and appeal. The crowd never knows what is going to happen next, and to tell you the truth, I don't think Jim does either." Neither one of us had taken our eyes off the stage. I added, "Jim's spontaneity is part of his creative drive. Sometimes I think some of his drinking is fueled by his desire to connect with the audience and *break on through* to another level of experience." Townsend nodded but I sensed he viewed my analysis with some skepticism and wasn't quite sure what to make of Jim. I discovered obvious images of that incident long after that day, as I listened to Townsend's lyrics in the song "Sally Simpson" from the rock opera *Tommy*. Whatever Pete's impression had been that day, Jim's charisma had gotten to him too.

The performance ended with the crowd charging the stage and the band fleeing under a hail of thrown debris. It was a wild and fitting ending, but on the way back to the hotel, it was clear that the other members of the band were disturbed and worried about Jim's onstage and offstage behavior. Everyone who knew Jim agreed that he was a complex person. He was painfully shy, vulnerable, gentle but also at times forceful, obstinate, and angry. Today, people often use the word *bipolar* to describe such dramatic differences in behavior, but I don't think applying that label gets to the essence of someone like Jim. We all share a capacity for contradictions and opposing emotions, but when a person is living under the lens of public scrutiny, the contrasts are magnified, creating both speculation and sensationalism. Jim was, and remains, a mystery. A profoundly human mystery with a tangled and intricate soul.

## Crazy in Cleveland

My standard strategy for trying to keep Jim away from distractions and alcohol before a show was a tight travel schedule, reducing the amount of dangerous downtime.

We flew nonstop from New York to Cleveland the next day, arriving a little after two in the afternoon, and went to our rooms to rest until six, when we had to leave for the auditorium. Around five-thirty, I thought I'd better check on Jim. He didn't answer his phone or respond to my knock on his hotel room door, so I went down to the bar. Sure enough, there he was, listening to an army vet relate war stories. Jim was enthralled, enjoying every macabre tale, and drunk. I tried to get him to leave the bar as diplomatically as possible, but he would have none of it.

"We've got plenty of time," he said. "The show doesn't start for a couple of hours."

"Yes, Jim, but we have to deal with rush-hour traffic," I said anxiously.

I pleaded with him until he finally agreed to leave—but only if he could bring along a six-pack. I managed to leave three beers on the curb as we got the into car to go to the show, but he quickly noticed half his bottles were missing and was furious. All the way to the show he berated me; who was I, what right did I have to take away his beer, how dare I do that, and so on. Running late, we got stuck in traffic, fortunately nowhere near a place to buy more beer.

We arrived at the arena a few minutes before the scheduled showtime, and I thought all my problems were solved, forgetting that people backstage were always eager to supply band members with drugs, alcohol, and more. They were the "candymen," and one of them had given Jim a bottle of Jack Daniels. I tried at first to cajole the bottle away from him, but he was chugging and pacing backstage like a madman. His anger was impossible to deal with, and rather than antagonize him any further, I left him to his demons.

The Doors usually took the stage together, but Ray was aware of Jim's condition and he, John, and Robby agreed that maybe the best thing to do was to take the stage without him and start the show with an instrumental version of "Break on Through."

Jim stumbled, shit-faced, onstage. One hand held his Jack Daniels and the other gave the finger to the audience. Holy shit, I thought, what are we in store for now? The band tried to cover up his incoherent shouts with reverb and feedbacks, but it only revved

Jim's anger. As the band played "Five to One," he complained to them that he couldn't hear himself. He demanded with them to tone down the music, and when that didn't happen, he lost it!

"If I can't hear myself, I'm gonna kill somebody!"

The band valiantly tried to cover for him and played on, but Jim staggered around the stage asking the audience for cigarettes and interrupting the band's musical solos with his screams and shouts. Finally, he tore off his coat and flung the coat—and himself—into the audience. He never hit the ground. Fans held him aloft, passing him along like a beach ball until he was rescued by security. He made it back to the stage, but he couldn't complete the show. The band finished "Light My Fire" without Jim and fled the stage as fans began throwing chairs at them and destroying everything in their wake. The show was a disaster, and once again, I couldn't escape the feeling that I could have done more to prevent it.

## Take the Money and Run

Back in June, a briefcase with twenty-five thousand dollars in cash was plopped down on my desk.

"Money doesn't talk, it swears!" Bob Dylan's lyrics were running through my head, and I had to agree with him. The money was delivered by a strange guy, heir to a big-money family, who wanted to promote a Doors and Airplane show. He claimed to be more interested in music than money, and I wondered if I could trust a promoter who wasn't interested in money. Promoters are always in it for the money.

I took the risk and told him he could promote a show in Philadelphia, August 4th, if he agreed to my conditions, which included another twenty-five thousand dollars in cash delivered to me before the show. "No problem," he assured me.

In Philly, the final show of the wild weekend tour ran smoothly, in sharp contrast to the Cleveland debacle the night before. The one glitch was a big one for me. I knew eighty percent of the tickets had been sold by noon the day of the concert, and I was concerned about my remaining $25,000. When I approached the wannabe promoter, he gave me $15,000 and claimed that was all he had. I immediately enlisted one of The Doors' security men, went into the box office, stood over the cashier, and took the remaining $10,000 from the door sales. It all went down very quickly. I knew what I had to do and did it.

The Doors went on late that night to a wildly cheering crowd and performed brilliantly. Jim was as sober as he was drunk the night before. They opened with "Back Door Man" followed by "Five to One."

Robby performed brilliantly on "Spanish Caravan," his flamenco-inspired piece, taking it to heights I had never heard before. The flamenco he had studied in his early guitar years showed in his performance. I felt Robbie was one of the most inventive and underrated guitar players of the 60s. He had his own nonderivative style, and I loved to listen to him. Perhaps because he was a quiet guy and Jim was the opposite, Robby was never given the credit he deserved, despite the fact that he was responsible for most of the music on "Light My Fire."

That night, Jim was nonconfrontational with his fans, singing their requests and taking beers and cigarettes from their outstretched hands. He recited poetry, danced like a shaman on fire, and captivated the audience with a beautifully controlled performance. It was a relief!

I left the City of Brotherly Love with a suitcase full of cash, grateful that the insane weekend had come to a close but knowing that the stress and anxiety had taken its toll.

## Turning the Page

When I returned from my exhausting weekend on the road, I met with David Baumgarten, who was anxious to hear about the money generated from the concerts and not at all interested in my personal tribulations. David had been in the entertainment business for many years and was first and foremost a businessman. Financial success was his number-one priority. As a player, though, he was experiencing problems. He was old school, and the rapid changes in business and society were making him feel uncomfortable not only with the new rock groups but also with many of the ideals and goals of my generation. I too wanted to make money and be successful professionally, but I also wanted something more, something that was evolving in my mind and heart but that I could not yet articulate.

One issue irked me when I returned to New York. The Doors and the Airplane were scheduled for a two-week European tour in September, and even though our agency wasn't contractually bound for concerts outside the United States, I wanted to accompany them. David refused my request. "You need to be in New York to focus your attention on other groups," he told me. He was referring to some of the other West Coast groups we had signed: Iron Butterfly, Love, and Steppenwolf. They were looking for work and wanted and expected from us what we had provided for The Doors and the Airplane. He was probably right from a strictly business point of view, but my point of view was outgrowing a "strictly business" perspective. To assuage my disappointment, he hinted at a big year-end bonus and added, "You can go to Europe next year with the Chambers Brothers."

I felt I was being underpaid in relation to the revenue I was bringing in, so I was pleased at the prospect of what I felt was a well-deserved bonus. However, working with the Chambers Brothers' manager was a nightmare. I was quickly reminded of that fact the next day, when their odious manager entered my office and declared, "Now that you won't be going to Europe with your favorite bands, you'll have time to put together a money-making tour for the Chambers Brothers next year."

My workload was so demanding that I didn't have time to stay mad. I had to book three East Coast shows for The Doors at the end of August, before their departure to Europe. When I said my good-byes to Jim and the band, I didn't realize it would be the last time I would ever see them. Life and careers would take us in different directions, but the time I spent with them is one of my cherished memories.

In late 1968, the world around me was exploding with historic events and exciting opportunities, and I was only too happy to be swept away by its promise and energy. I had a growing sense that my ambitions and ideals would carve a unique path, and I was eager to see what that would be.

# CHAPTER 8

## SHARK BAIT

"Didn't recognize me, did ya?"

Hell no! A guy was standing in my office doorway, and I didn't have a clue *who* he was. He was an average height, nearly bald, sporting a mustache, and wearing a tan trench coat. He approached and extended his hand, "Bob Darin."

Splish Splash! Could it be Bobby Darin? Bobby "Mack the Knife" Darin? Then he smiled and there was no question. He was *that* Bobby Darin. I couldn't believe that he was standing in front of me. I was starstruck.

Seeing him transported me back eight years to the evening of my senior prom; Bobby D was appearing at the Copacabana Club in New York City. My dad, who was in the wine business, had a connection and got me a table in the rear to see the show. Back then, Sinatra was still the rage for my parents' generation, but we were cruisin' to the hipper pre-rock sixties sounds of Elvis, Fats Domino, and the Everly Brothers and vocal quartets such as the Drifters and the Platters. But Bobby Darin was in a class all his own. He was the late fifties-early sixties hipster who took us from Sinatra to the vitality of rock 'n' roll with "Mack the Knife," "Dream Lover," "Artificial Flowers," and "Beyond the Sea."

In June 1960, Darin was making his debut at the Copa. I was just eighteen, but being at the Copa made me feel like an important adult. I can imagine how I must have appeared in my rented tuxedo with my date in her prom gown. We were a couple of clueless kids, gaga with excitement but acting as grown-up as we could, sipping our mixed drinks as we waited for Bobby to take the stage. Darin was a huge crossover star, with an adult as well as teen fan base, and both crowds were out in full.

The place was jam-packed and the feeling of expectation at Darin's imminent appearance was electric. After what felt like an endless wait, he charged on stage, self-assured, and was welcomed by a thunderous ovation. He jumped right into his finger-snapping, syncopated rhythmic style. A master of multiple genres, he danced, joked, and gave deft impressions. He was dazzling as he moved from one hit song to another with a pop dynamism that eclipsed—even to this day—anything I'd ever experienced. Sammy Davis, Jr., said that Darin was the only act he would never follow on stage. After seeing the performance that night, I could see why.

"I'm making a career change," Darin said, shaking me out of my reverie and back to the present. "Direction Records is my new company," Darin continued. "We're gonna put out folk and protest music. I've got a new album that's just come out with my own songs, and I want to do some concerts," he said, handing me the LP. "I hear you're the guy that books these new bands."

I was taken aback. It felt more like a command than a request. It was as if it was a foregone conclusion that I was going to do what he wanted me to do. He was trying to be humble but his big exploding ego belied his faux humble pose.

I wasn't particularly taken with the look of the album. At first glance, it seemed to me that he was trying to reinvent himself in an effort to capitalize on rock's emerging political agenda, and I recalled reading that he had been with Robert Kennedy on the '68 presidential campaign trail. He pressed on. "All topical stuff—you'll like it. I produced it, arranged it, wrote all the songs—cover design, pictures—did it all myself."

God was he intense! I was getting a glimpse now of the fervently driven man behind the performer at the Copa. I could only imagine how it would be to work for this guy. "Why are you choosing to make such an abrupt change in your public persona?" I asked.

"Times they are a-changin'," he smirked, "and I feel I have something to contribute." He calmed down and the tone of the meeting began to change as he explained how he had done some soul searching while working for Bobby Kennedy and was feeling a connection with the counterculture movement. It had spurred him to write topical songs that reflected this newfound connection and voiced his thoughts on the social and political issues dividing the nation. "I saw Bobby take it in the head and go down. You have no idea how witnessing that assassination affected me. I was so devastated that it drove me into seclusion," he explained. "I needed to channel my feelings of despair at his loss, express how I felt, and these songs just . . . just poured out of me."

While my first inclination had been to dismiss him as a disingenuous opportunist, his candor was quickly winning me over. I, too, had experienced a deep depression over Robert Kennedy's death and could relate to his desire to make a contribution. He was proud of his achievement and eager to get on the road. We stood, and I took a moment to tell him I loved his show at the Copa. He gave me that Darin smile and pointed to the LP on the desk. "Listen to the album. I know you'll come up with some creative performance ideas. I work fast and can put a band together in no time. I'll call you in a few days. Let me know what you think." He delivered his thoughts in what seemed like one breath. He extended his hand and said, "Gotta go. Nice to meet you." Then he spun around and walked out the door in a flash.

Whew! I sat back in my chair, took a deep breath, and thought —what just happened? I got up and closed the door, then went over to the player to put on the record. I pulled out the lyric sheet, sat down, and listened to the album. It wasn't Dylan, but the songs poetically brought to light the broader endemic ills that faced our country. It was more than just a protest album. It was a sensitive and truly heartfelt songwriter's first attempt at cathartic songwriting.

I never heard from him again. I don't know why. I thought about trying to locate him, but after mentioning the meeting to David Baumgarten, I abandoned the idea. David said to forget about him. He knew Darin had agency representation elsewhere for his nightclub and movie activities and that that was where the money was. He said his agent probably didn't want to expend the effort to book him into low-paying folk clubs and had tried to talk him out of it. "No doubt, he was unable to convince his manager of his career change ambitions, and he came to you, hoping you'd work hard for little money." David added, "Nightclubs are where he belongs and where he should stay. Anyway, I heard he's a real pain in the ass to work for." Here was a perfect example of how management can stifle an artist's creativity in the money game. That's what the "business" is all about. I was learning fast.

Bobby played the Troubadour in LA and a couple of other clubs in 1969 but soon put his toupee back on, shaved his mustache, and returned to TV, movies, and nightclubs, slipping a few of his new songs into the repertoire here and there. Protest songs didn't go over big in Vegas—at least not in 1970.

> *Oh, the shark, babe, has such teeth, dear*
> *And it shows them pearly white*
> *Showbiz put a knife in Bobby' plans, babe,*
> *And kept that album out of sight.*

# CHAPTER 9

## SLICK MOVES

"Hello, you fools! You've got Rembrandts over the mantle and a Rolls in the garage, but your old man wouldn't know a clitoris from a junk bond—if you had the guts to show him your twat in the first place!"

My jaw dropped when I heard Grace Slick's opening salvo. I was having a polite conversation with Jorma Kaukonen, Sr., the father of Jefferson Airplane's lead guitarist. Jorma, Sr., was a dignified, erudite gentleman whose thoughts and opinions I enjoyed hearing. Our civilized exchange was a stark contrast to the shocking remarks blasting over the sound system, and we looked at each other in surprised and amused disbelief. It wasn't that it was unusual for Grace, the Jefferson Airplane's diva, to open a show with an obscenity-laced diatribe, but the setting tonight—the stage of New York City's prestigious Whitney Museum of American Art—was a backdrop that seemed to make her remarks stand out more than usual.

The au courant and ever-edgy Whitney had invited Glenn McKay to stage an exhibition of the light show performance art he had developed as a psychedelic accompaniment to the sights and sounds of San Francisco–based bands and Ken Kesey's "acid tests." Glenn described his fluid, abstract, illuminated imagery as an art form that provided a new door to the consciousness of sound and color—so in touch with the emotion and the rhythm of the experience that all sense of separation between color, moving images, and sound melted away.

Appreciating the total sensory immersion that Glenn's art offered required the accompaniment of a trippy West Coast band, and he had invited his pioneering artist friends, Jefferson Airplane, to help demonstrate his hybrid of art and entertainment. The event was attended by the Friends of the Whitney, the blue chip, in-the-know, diamond-and-fur crowd who donated big bucks to the arts.

Grace, well loosened by the disinhibiting effects of her alcohol of choice that evening, was greeting the august assembly as they filed into the auditorium and expressing her heartfelt opinions on Gucci loafers, diamond rings, and tight girdles. She excoriated the habitually flattered and fawned-over connoisseurs of culture, who were not sure what to make of Grace's monologues. Was it free verse irony? Metaphorical juxtaposition? Dada? In the halls of high art, one never knew if true art wasn't mischievously disguised as the ridiculous. One thing was certain. In the pantheon of rock divas, Grace Slick was one of the first and one of the badass best.

Born Grace Wing to a wealthy West Coast family, she was educated in private schools and graduated from Finch College in New York City, where she rubbed shoulders and other body parts with the upper crust. She found her true calling, however, in the rough-and-tumble world of rock, where she proved she could tumble as well as anyone. In addition to belting out legendary hits, Grace delivered some of the era's most obscene, sarcastic, and ear-withering commentary. Her special target was anyone with a sense of propriety who could be offended or shocked. I'd seen her strip to the waist during an outdoor concert in the rain because she didn't want to get her blouse wet. At a show in Fort Wayne, Indiana, she studied the crowd and asked, "Which of you has the biggest cock?" The audience seemed puzzled, as if she had confused Hoosier with hoser.

As a former member of the social elite, Grace felt strongly motivated to show her disgust for what she perceived to be their pretensions and arrogance. Raw, spontaneous, and passionate, she was rebelling against values and attitudes she had come to despise. Now, at the ever-chic Whitney, in front of her one-time social peers, the rock star queen was publicly demonstrating her disdain for her socialite past.

A strong, smart, and talented woman, Grace was a protofeminist in the days of the Whitney event. She demanded the right to act, think, and express herself as she saw fit. Her remarks could be clever and witty, but when she'd been drinking, which was often, she would simply berate people with scalding invectives and crude insults. She didn't tolerate fools or trite questions from the press, and if asked to describe her singing style, she would invariably reply, "Loud." When one naïve reporter asked, "How did you write *White Rabbit?*" she shot back, "With a pencil on paper." But crude or clever, Grace was always entertaining, and the band and the Airplane entourage were loyal and supportive of the feelings she voiced, which were genuine and deeply felt.

One of the sound technicians working at the show that night had given Grace a new electronic innovation at the time, a cordless microphone. Grace—quick to abuse this liberating device—was off and running. She called it "warming up the straights." My agency and I had no working relationship with the event, and I was there as a guest of the band. I had covered many Airplane concerts in the past and had come to enjoy Grace's offstage wit and off-color performance theatrics, but tonight, under the circumstance, I wondered if their manager was finding Grace's impromptu rants alarming and uncomfortable. I searched out Bill to get his take.

"She's on a roll tonight," he shrugged, bemused and stoic. "A minute ago, she was introduced to the curator's wife, and she asked the woman if she was really fucking him or just living off his prestige."

Meanwhile, on stage, Grace paused to catch her breath and the band took it as a cue to rock the joint. Glenn projected his strobe lights and special effects and the music took over. Feeding off the energy of Grace's purged emotions, the band gave the crowd at the Whitney everything they had hoped for and more.

It was raw and real, and the music and lights were conspiring to take the audience's heightened sensibilities to a new, experimental, and exciting dimension of art and consciousness. However, Grace felt it necessary to distill this new consciousness with her intoxicated free verse. Slurring her words during a mid-song monologue, she addressed the crowd derogatorily as "filthy jewels," which with the distortion sounded to many like "filthy Jews." It came across as an intentionally egregious slight, and the members of the band were motionless in the background, outwardly uncomfortable but inwardly relishing Grace's blasphemous outspokenness.

By the end of the night, tuxedoes and designer gowns were swaying and dancing to the beat. As usual, the party ran late, but the crowd seemed energized by the event. On my way out, walking behind two elegantly attired, slightly tipsy mavens, I heard one exclaim, "I just love the spontaneity of the avant-garde, and that Grace woman is a stitch, but tell me, dear, what in the world is a twat?"

# CHAPTER 10

# ROOFTOP REVOLUTIONARIES

I heard the thumping of heavy footsteps on the stairs and spun around as the door flew open and a squad of cops spilled out onto the rooftop. We were busted!

It was pandemonium on the roof of the Schuyler Hotel on Forty-fifth Street in Manhattan that cold November day in 1968. Roadies, cameramen, musicians, girlfriends, and guests of the recently enlisted members of the countercultural revolution scattered. Grace Slick, standing in for Liberty leading the people, was dancing a jig in exaltation at the edge of the rooftop. The police were surprised by the musicians and camera crew, and I escaped to join Grace at the roof's edge. We looked down gleefully at the street below, where more cops were attempting to control the crowd that had gathered. Traffic was backed up, cars were honking, and the screams of approaching police sirens were adding to the chaos. The cameramen, undeterred by the police, were catching the action from all angles as the noise and confusion continued to escalate. "Who's in charge? Where are your permits?" the blue meanies demanded.

Marty Balin, the Airplane's vocalist, joined us at the edge of the roof. Fired up with revolutionary passion, he screamed, "Wake up, New York! Wake up, you fuckers! Free music! Free love!" The police had their man or, at least, someone they could arrest.

## High Notes

The impromptu Jefferson Airplane hotel rooftop concert had been staged with a film project the band was working on with the internationally celebrated New Wave film director and political radical Jean-Luc Godard. I had been tipped off about the event by Bill Thompson and was there to check out the happening.

Godard had become increasingly strident in his passion for left-wing politics. He was fashioning a Counter Cinema movement that sought to use film as an agent to bring attention to the cultural brainwashing of conventional films and to create a new political-social consciousness. He didn't want to entertain audiences; he wanted to startle them out of their bourgeois, consumer trance. In New York to shoot footage for his film tentatively titled *One A.M. (One American Movie)*, Godard had met members of the Airplane in the cultural cauldron of the city's social scene. The Airplane admired his creative audacity, social convictions, and experimental approach, and they'd agreed to be part of his free-form guerilla film. It was to be shot in traditional revolutionary style, and the rooftop performance was unannounced and unauthorized. The movie was unscripted, but the filming of the rooftop scene was well planned. Documentary director D. A. Pennebaker, best known for his Dylan film *Don't Look Back,* had his camera set up across the street with mobile cameramen stationed on the street and on the hotel roof to capture the effect of hand-held camera realism. When the band started playing, workers streamed out onto the sidewalks and streets looking skyward, congesting traffic and creating what the police later called a "public disturbance."

Godard's plan was for the band to do their own thing on the roof, reminiscent of his improvised *Sympathy for the Devil* film with the Rolling Stones. In the hotel on the floor below, actors Paula Matter and Rip Torn were set to peer out the window in feigned astonishment when the music started. To give it that edgy, avant-garde panache, Matter was naked under a sheet and the notoriously over-the-top Rip Torn, sporting a flamboyant red scarf, was poised to give it his exaggerated best. Everybody was working for free, and the whole setup felt like an anarchist's prank.

On Marty's cue, the guitars began to wail, the drums pounded out the beat, and Grace whirled and sang on the rooftop stage high above the streets. Below, the citizens of New York played their parts, as did the city's finest. Rip Torn, going for an underground Oscar in that flowing red scarf, had pushed himself into the center of the fray, demanding that the "people's concert" should go on. He smiled triumphantly when he was handcuffed and placed beside Marty in the back of a police cruiser, as roving cameras filmed the arrest of the celebrity dissidents.

The cops ordered the band to pack up, which they were happy to do. They had completed their mission, and it was growing colder on the roof. The police seemed satisfied as well. They had broken up the rebels' concert and had two counterculture hero-martyrs under arrest. It had been a good little war. The reaction of the crowd in the street ranged from "Wow, how cool!" from the younger workers, happy for a brief respite from work, to "What a disgrace!" from disgruntled old harrumphers. I wondered where Monsieur Jean-Luc Godard—the mastermind, the provocateur, the Che of the counter-cinema—was in the midst of this inspired chaos? Had he escaped to the mountains, the jungle, the caves? Apparently, he was in one of the nearby high-rises, watching the fray from above, no doubt amused by his creation and relishing his success from a safe vantage point. As for *One A.M.,* Godard eventually abandoned the project.

His footage and his rambling film interviews with political radicals Tom Hayden and Eldridge Cleaver were eventually edited and assembled by D. A. Pennebaker, and *One A.M.* appropriately premiered in December of 1969 in an art house in Berkeley, California. The film never obtained distribution and is now out of circulation.

I did not possess the revolutionary zeal of many in the rebellious youth culture who actively supported the civil rights movement and demonstrated against the Vietnam War in the sixties. Yet, returning to my office late that afternoon, I felt gratified that even though the event was farcical on many levels, my voice had been a small part of that large choir whose shouts and songs were the anthem of our hopes for a better world.

# CHAPTER 11

# CRISIS AND CHANGE

I envisioned myself, smiling and nodding, accepting my generous year-end bonus check from David Baumgarten. "David, you don't know what this means to me. It's not just the money. It's the respect and appreciation it represents. Truly, thank you!"

The moment had arrived. David handed me the check, and as I glanced at the amount, my imagined words of gratitude were transformed into sheer speechlessness. Five hundred dollars! I was expecting a pat on the back, not a slap in the face! Stunned, I got up and walked toward the door. Seeing my disappointment, David maneuvered out from behind his desk and caught up with me. "Richard, you have a big future at APA. Be patient. There's a vice presidency waiting for you."

APA had capitalized on the exploding popularity of rock, demonstrated by its prestigious list of clients headed by The Doors and Jefferson Airplane. The rapid expansion of the rock division— of which I was the original and sole New York member—had grown to five full-time agents. My piddling salary of one hundred fifty dollars a week did not reflect this financial boom, and the meager bonus only fueled my discontent with APA and my irritation with David, which had been escalating since his refusal to send me on The Doors-Jefferson Airplane European tour.

David knew my frustrations and had been hearing my complaints for some time but always gave me the same answer: "I will make it up to you." Now he was making more promises— promises, promises, and more promises!

It was December 1968. The year had been hectic and stressful, and I was hoping it would end on a satisfying note. The paltry bonus check had dealt a nasty blow, but I tried once again to convince myself that my time would come. Despite my efforts, I was also haunted by a lingering discontent with a source deeper than a lack of financial compensation. It wasn't just APA; I had placed my trust in the entire system but was beginning to question its validity. The "work your way up" mentality was the business mantra I had accepted and adopted. Now I found myself wondering where I was working my way up to—and—did I really want to go there?

## Tripping the Switch

"Wanna try a hit of this here acid? It's really good." "Sure, why not," I said, and took a tab from one of the California guys on the road crew.

Destiny can find you no matter where you are. I was in Cologne, Germany. It was February 1969, and I was accompanying the Chambers Brothers on a short European tour. The doubts and anxieties that had begun to weigh heavily on me during the winter were increasing, and I was feeling desperately unhappy. I was hoping the psychedelic and a long walk along the Rhine might provide a momentary respite and lighten my spirits.

The tour had been ill advised from the start. Under pressure from the group's surly manager, my boss had instructed me to put something together for them in London and on the Continent. They were not well known by rock fans in the UK and Europe, so promoters were not eager to book them. I'd been able to arrange only a couple of shows in London, a show in Stockholm, and four gigs in Germany. It was the first time the Chambers Brothers would be playing outside the United States, and they were excited and looking forward to the tour. Their manager, instead of being grateful for my efforts, was condescending, irrational, and unjustly critical. He took every opportunity to berate me, and kept accusing me of favoring The Doors and Airplane over the Chambers Brothers. "Why don't we have more shows in England? Why don't we have more TV exposure? How many shows did The Doors do? The promoters aren't spending enough on publicity." I'd worked diligently for the band for close to two years, most of that time before they even had a manager. I believed in them and liked their music, and they knew it.

The Chambers Brothers always put on exceptionally high-spirited performances, and in Europe they were feted with standing ovations at every show. I was happy for them, but the behind-the-scenes tensions were, for me, becoming unsustainable. When the guy on the road crew offered me a hit of LSD from his stash, I thought it might be just the thing to relieve my stress. The road crew were veteran users and never performance impaired. "Is it strong?" I asked, apprehensively studying the innocuous-looking little tab.

"Nah, only a hundred or so milligrams. You'll barely get a toasting." What the hell, I thought. I swallowed it and started walking the streets alone. I had never taken acid before and was expecting a kind of trippy, enhanced marijuana high—something that would lift my spirits without blowing my mind. It didn't take long before I could feel the blood coursing through my veins. Everything and everybody around me was sparkly and surreal. I found myself on a bench in front of a huge, glorious Gothic cathedral with monumental spires. I had no idea how I'd arrived there, but there it was: shimmering, alive, and frightening in its jaw-dropping magnificence and immensity. I'd never seen anything remotely like it in my life. My first acid trip was a life-altering experience. I was physically seated in front of the magnificent cathedral, but my inner self was entering an alternative space of introspection and revelation. I lost track of time and place, but when my consciousness returned to that cathedral bench, I realized I had to quit the tour and my job to search for a more authentic life. This time, when I asked myself if I truly wanted a career in the agency business, the answer was crystal clear—FUCK NO!

With indubitable certainty, I knew that cajoling, maneuvering, and babysitting clients and competing for favor in a cutthroat business wouldn't bring me the joy I was seeking. I was just twenty-six, and I wanted out. I wanted to be free to travel, to experience life. Some might question my judgment, making such an important decision as result of an LSD trip, but I equate it to a kind of shamanic vision that gave me the impetus to transition to another life phase. Forty-five years later, I have never regretted my decision, although one acid trip did not solve *all* my problems. As the acid started wearing off, I returned to the hotel with an exuberance that I hadn't felt in years. I had made my decision: I was quitting the agency, selling what I owned, and starting a new life in Europe. My plan was not well thought out, but I trusted that the Universe would provide and felt elated with a self-liberating burst of energy.

The next day, I called in my resignation to the head of the concert department at APA. Initially, he refused to accept it and tried as best he could to accentuate my accomplishments and placate my discontent. The more he spoke, the more resolute I became. He said a raise was forthcoming, but I'd heard that before and I no longer saw money and a vice presidency as measures of success. I was done with the ruthless competition of the agency business and the ethical duplicities it demanded. I was not the fresh-faced kid they'd hired nearly three years ago. I'd been spending a lot of time getting high with artists, and my sensibilities had been transformed. I'd stopped measuring success with the same yardstick and was unwilling to surrender my ethical values for the job or pay in stress for the trappings of affluence. I was unsure where my bold decision would ultimately lead, but I was invigorated and committed to a new direction in life.

# Chapter 12

## Interlude

"Where are you from?"

"The U.S."

The Dutch cop was sizing me up: long hair, weird clothes, and a foreigner. Outside the police station, other cops were searching my Fiat.

"What are you doing in Amsterdam?"

"Visiting friends."

"Where are you going?"

"To my friends' home in Tilburg."

"Where did you meet your friends?"

"In Paris. They invited me to visit them."

"Where were you before Paris?"

"Italy, England, the Alps, France."

"Tourist?"

"Visitor."

He gave me a questioning look. I said, "My family is Italian and I have a place near Turin."

"How long do you plan to stay in Holland?"

Plan? I didn't have a plan! That was the whole point. I had quit my job and embarked on a journey with no planned destination or time frame.

After resigning from the agency in Germany, I returned to the States and shocked my parents with the news that I'd quit. I sold my possessions, gave up my Greenwich Village digs, and followed the dictum of the day: "Turn on, tune in, drop out." A friend of my father's was in the import business and was able to secure free transportation for me on a freighter bound for Genoa, Italy. He also owned a small apartment in a little village in his old hometown, not far from Turin, where I set up a base of operations.

The cop was waiting for an answer when another officer entered the room and said something to him in Dutch. He stood and motioned toward the door. "All right, you're free to go." It was my turn to give him the questioning look. "The reason we stopped you," he explained, "is because there have been some burglaries in the area and we are checking on any . . . uh, strangers." Yeah, sure.

I wasn't in any position to complain. I had a stash of cannabis in my pocket and was lucky they had searched the car and not me. I continued on my journey, following whatever touched my heart or caught my imagination.

## The Secret of Zed Habab

I liked to drink cappuccinos in the outside cafés and listen to the stories of other travelers and exotic characters who seemed to materialize, now that I'd stepped outside the mainstream to meander life's unmapped side roads. I was sitting in the plaza in Ivrea, a town not far from my village, when Said appeared out of the dark shadows cast by the warm, bright Italian sun. No traveler was more entertaining than Said. He had an air of mystery I did not want to puncture by questioning the veracity of his exploits and adventures. True or false, they were enormously entertaining.

Said was Egyptian and a few years older than I. He claimed he'd been a captain in the Egyptian military and was AWOL. He was working for Olivetti, a typewriter and telecommunication company, in Ivrea, where he said he ran some sort of language translation machine. As I got to know him, he regaled me with tales of secret missions in the military that had demanded specially trained operatives.

We stepped into the privacy of the nearby alley and shared some good California weed before returning to our table. Said liked a good smoke, and it seemed to enhance his storytelling proclivity. "What'd you think of the smoke?" I asked, feeling pleasantly stoned.

"It's like a nice, light wine," he said. "Good for an afternoon puff."

"Yeah, you can still function," I agreed, "not like some of that Pakistani hash I've smoked."

Never to be outdone, Said nodded, "Yes, but the real king is zed habab." I knew that Said had traveled extensively, spoke several Middle Eastern languages, and loved his smoke, so I had to ask.

"What's that?"

"Oh, my friend, zed habab is the smoker's holy grail."

Who knew? "Okay, Said. You got me. What is that shit?"

"It's made only in Lebanon, in the Bekaa Valley, from *Cannabis indica*, a different strain than your *Cannabis sativa*. They have perfected a centuries-old method of extracting the oil to create a smoke"—he leaned over and looked into my eyes—"that is smooth, strong, and takes your senses to another dimension." Ooh . . . I hadn't even had a puff of zed habab and already I had visions of a cannabis crusade. Once I found this magic substance, I would share it with potheads in the western world. I would be well-beloved—and filthy rich!

## The Road to Lebanon

After a couple of nights drinking wine and smoking weed, I had figured out my strategy and invited Said over to hear it. "I'll pack the Fiat with all my typical tourist gear . . ."

"Right, right." Said nodded. "Just another dumb American tourist. No offense."

I raved on, "I'll leave Turin, go east to Trieste, then down the Adriatic coast to Dubrovnik, over to Greece, down to Piraeus, book passage to Lebanon, and I'm there."

"Piece of cake."

"I'll drive to the Bekaa Valley and hang out with the locals till I make the right connection. Then I'll take this syringe" (I held up a large hypodermic) "and puncture these fruit juice cans, refill them with hash oil, solder the cans closed, and reglue the labels."

"Genius!" Said exclaimed.

My plan was in fact idiotic, but I was under the intoxicating spell of the legend of zed habab, and common sense was not an antidote.

I left Italy, drove along the Adriatic, slept on the beach, swam in the calm sea, ate freshly caught fish, mingled with the locals, and had a grand time. I got swept up in the beauty of the coastline and the joy of travel. My secret mission added a delicious note of intrigue to the journey. After Dubrovnik, I drove east over miles of dirt roads through Montenegro, toward a little village in Kosovo called Peć. The road wound through mountains where the only person I encountered for miles was a man guiding a donkey-drawn cart filled with cut wood. The road was in such poor condition that I had to cut the trembling old Fiat down to five miles an hour. It was nearly dark when I arrived at the remote hamlet of Peć, exhausted and hungry.

The village appeared closed down for the night. Tired, hungry, and alone, the romance of travel was quickly fading. If I couldn't find food or shelter, maybe I could at least beg a drink of water. I rumbled past the quiet cottages in the darkening light until I came across a small building that looked like it was a small inn or cafe. Seeing a light within, I parked and tentatively knocked. An older man, wearing a white shirt, black vest, and white Turkish-style turban, answered my knock. He gave me a welcoming smile and motioned me inside, where a woman in peasant attire was equally as friendly. With no common language, I mimed bringing food to my mouth and they nodded.

Fortunately, these kind folks took pity on me, fed me, and put me up for the night. This simple episode illustrated one of the great lessons that travel can bestow, the universality of human kindness. When you are the recipient, it is a humbling and soul-enriching experience.

Two days later, I finally arrived in Piraeus and booked passage to Beirut, the land of the fabled zed habab.

## Dark Freighter to the Green Hills

The *Felix Dzerzhinsky* was a drab, hulking World War II freighter disguised as a passenger liner. Once onboard, I realized why it offered the cheapest passage to Lebanon. It was a ghost ship.

It had been one of several Gulag slave ships employed some thirty or more years ago by Stalin to transport over a million prisoners to remote locations in Siberia. Lying awake in my tiny, gray, windowless room on a hard bed, I imagined every creak and groan of the old ship to be the haunted echoes of its doomed human cargo steaming toward their deaths.

After a sleepless night, I sat on the deck watching my fellow passengers, most of whom were from the Soviet Union, bound for a late summer holiday in Latakia, Syria. As the Russian-speaking men and women dressed in shades of gray crisscrossed in front of me, I imagined myself a foreign agent in some Cold War novel who was about to be exposed and tortured. I could hear myself screaming, "I'm not a spy! I'm just a fuckin' smuggler for Chrissakes!"

"Excuse me, my friend, I couldn't help but notice that you seem a little uncomfortable." I looked up at the smiling face of a casually dressed Middle Eastern man in his mid-thirties.

"Who me? Uncomfortable?"

Mounir Najem laughed and introduced himself. He was returning home to Lebanon from Paris, where he had recently attended an exhibit of his paintings. Mounir was cultured, educated, and amiable. We quickly became traveling companions, which greatly reduced my anxiety level on this death-ship voyage. Mounir's family had a small hotel in his hometown of Deir el Qamar, situated in the cool Lebanese mountains twenty minutes from Beirut. Because I had a vehicle, he suggested that I stay there rather than Beirut, which was hot in the summer months.

True to his word, the hotel was a divine place located in the hills leading to Mount Lebanon and operated by his beautiful and gracious sister, Mona. I was now within forty miles of zed habab.

## Smoke Dreams

The morning after I arrived at the hotel, I was up early and anxious to get started on my road trip. I told my hosts that I was driving to the Roman temples at Baalbek for the day, but my real destination was the Bekaa Valley, where I prayed I would complete my pilgrimage.

I drove east on the Beirut-Damascus highway and turned north until I reached Zahlé, the main city in the Bekaa. I passed through this red-roofed village in the foothills of Mount Sannine and continued north, driving through fields of sunflowers, until I came to a small settlement nestled in the foothills. I parked outside the village store, where I thought I could have a cup of tea and perhaps get a sense of the local scene. Inside, I was promptly approached by a man in his mid-thirties who looked businesslike, dressed neatly in dark trousers and a white shirt. "Hashish?" he asked. My cool facade was immediately blown. You go to the vineyards for wine, the orchards for fruit, and apparently as everyone but I knew, to the goddamn Bekaa Valley for hash. His poor English with a French accent was enough to conduct business. "Come," said the stranger, and I followed him down the dirt road to what I hoped would be the gates to zed habab.

He chatted in his combination of French and broken English as he led me directly to a small veranda that overlooked a beautiful vegetable garden. There, in close proximity, was a small field of neatly spaced four-foot-high cannabis plants. I smiled in admiration while he removed a small piece of hash from his pocket, crumpled it into a pipe, and handed it to me. The hash was fragrant and produced a nice buzz.

He motioned for me to follow him to a crude barnlike building. Inside, several young Arabs were processing bundles of cannabis by sieving them over and over until the plant was reduced to a resinous powder that they would manually compress. He explained by pointing to the bundles of weed and then to the hash that it took

**97**

fifty kilos of the dried plants to produce a one-kilo brick of primo blonde Lebanese hash. "You buy?" he asked.

"Do you have hashish oil?"

"*Non, pas d'huile.* No hash oil," he responded, shaking both hands above his shoulders.

"Zed habab?"

"Who is zed habab?" he asked.

The hash was good, but I hadn't come all this way for hash; besides, I had no way to safely transport kilos of bulky hash back to Europe. I told him I didn't have any money on me but would return the next day. Not wanting to lose a sale, he said, "Best quality. Good price for you." I was amazed how quickly his English improved when it came to making a deal. I bought a freshly made piece and begged off on any more, promising I'd return.

Before I resumed my search, I decided it would be best to discreetly ask Mounir if he knew anything about hash oil. Mounir was born and raised in Deir el Qamar and would surely know the lay of the land.

Indeed, Mounir did know a thing or two about buying and smuggling hash. "Do you want to be gang-raped and spend the rest of your life in jail?" he yelled at me. Those experiences were not on my travel must-do list. Mounir's cautionary remarks were making a definite impression. "Don't you understand?" Mounir screamed. "You can't trust those people. They are dishonest. They will sell you hash, take your money, and then report you to the police, who will intercept you on the road and arrest you. The police pay the growers to inform them!"

"But . . . what about zed habab?"

"For you, my friend, zed habab is just another word for suicide!"

I abandoned my crusade to the holy land and, even though I had not secured the smoker's holy grail, I felt I had been saved—from my own stupidity. I returned to Italy empty-handed but with a lifetime's stash of memories.

## An Itch for Action

My year in Italy connected me to the rich Italian heritage of my father and forefathers. I traveled the land, bathed in the sea, spoke the language, ate the food, soaked up the arts, and engaged the people. At twenty-seven, though, I was growing antsy and starting to miss the excitement that had been so much a part of my life a year ago.

I was keeping abreast of the music scene on Radio Luxembourg and driving to Turin to pick up the latest rock albums. *Abbey Road, Let It Bleed, Live/Dead, Tommy,* and Jefferson Airplane's *Volunteers* all connected me to my compatriots back home. I was having severe cultural and musical withdrawal, and listening to the music that spoke of my contemporaries' discontent made me want to go home and reconnect with members of my own generation.

I booked passage on a Costa Line freighter to New York and sold everything I had acquired during my European hiatus. I was excited to be returning to the United States but felt a little apprehensive. Somewhere along the way, maybe in a village in Kosovo or on a ghost ship to Lebanon, I had learned that in life's confusion, there comes a moment, seemingly random but strangely meaningful, that will lead to new and brighter horizons.

# CHAPTER 13

# A SIMPLE TWIST OF FATE

Spring 1970, I was walking the streets of Greenwich Village and trying to answer the puzzle of my life. I was living with friends in a loft in SoHo and had no clue what I was going to do next. Even though I had quit the music business, I still had a passion for music. I was broke and needed a job, but going back into the music business under the same circumstances that had driven me crazy and caused me to quit was not an option.

Stymied by what to do, I just wanted to walk, enjoy the spring weather, and clear my head. Crossing the street, I was jolted out of my thoughts. "Hey, is that you, David?"

"Richard!" It was David Grisman. "What're you doin', man? Long time, no see!" It was unbelievable running into David out of the blue like that! He was equally surprised, and we were excited to see each other.

David, arguably the finest mandolin player this side of Bill Monroe, was also a superb record producer, engineer, and music arranger. We had been friends since 1967, when he was a member of the Earth Opera band with Peter Rowan. Peter was a talented singer and musician who eventually achieved great success on the folk-country circuit. Earth Opera was trying to make it as a rock band. Jac Holzman, the president of Elektra Records, had signed them to his label and asked me to help promote them. Despite some limited success, Earth Opera never caught on and disbanded while I was out of the country.

David lived nearby and invited me over to his apartment to catch up on things. We rolled a big one and settled in. I quickly learned that he, too, was burned out by the music industry bullshit and no longer interested in the underground rock movement. He was trying to promote Peter Rowan's younger brothers, Chris and Lorin. They were both gifted songwriters and had the good looks and sweet harmonies that young female record buyers loved. I listened to a couple of cuts he'd made of their music and agreed that they had rich potential.

The more we talked, the more excited we became. In a matter of hours, we had formed Hieronymusic, a management-production company with clear-cut goals—get the Rowan Brothers a record deal, make a hit single, and get rich.

The confusion that had plagued me hours before was replaced with the excitement of new prospects. Was running into David a stroke of luck or something else? My ongoing curiosity about how and why things happen was once again sparked. Whether luck, destiny, coincidence, synchronicity, or the alignment of the stars was involved, I was intrigued and grateful.

After we agreed to form the partnership, David and I were pretty much inseparable. We worked hard to promote the venture and focused attention on the musical and everyday needs of the Rowans. They were just kids; Lorin was barely out of high school and Chris was just a few years older. We pooled some money to support them while they concentrated on their music.

I rented a small apartment near David for my live-in office and started to put out feelers to land a record deal. David helped the guys shape their songs and provided musical guidance. In the three months that followed, the four of us enjoyed getting to know each other and took lots of psychedelics. We embarked on a collective effort to get physically fit and adopted a health rejuvenation program that included yoga and a macrobiotic brown rice food regimen. We were a fun-loving, high-spirited, optimistic bunch, working hard on our goals and hoping to break into the big time.

## Go West, Young Man

"Hey, let's go see Jerry."

Alright! David didn't need to twist my arm! I was excited about meeting Jerry Garcia. The Grateful Dead's *Workingman's Dead* album had come out around the time David and I started our partnership, and we had listened to it together. It was a departure from previous Dead record offerings, more akin to Jerry and David's roots in bluegrass and country and focused more on vocal arrangements than instrumental experimentation. We both liked the album and the direction the band was taking.

David's connection to Jerry went back to the early sixties, when the two then-unknown musicians met in a parking lot after a bluegrass festival. Jerry had heard David playing his mandolin in the back of a pickup truck and joined him on his banjo. Again, one of those fortuitous events that shape life.

David had just heard about an upcoming Dead show at the Fillmore East and immediately got on the phone to the Chelsea Hotel, where he'd heard Jerry was staying. He managed to get hold of his old friend, who said he'd leave a couple of comp tickets and backstage passes for us at the box office. The next night, the Fillmore East lobby was packed with tie-dyed Deadheads, and the air was heavy with the sweet aroma of cannabis. I was getting stoned on the vibes and feeling good when I heard, "Hey, Richard, looking to get back into the business? Europe not good enough for you, eh?"

It was Bill Graham. He had transformed the once dumpy and decrepit theater into a rock landmark and was justly proud of his accomplishment. We chatted briefly before he ran off to deal with one of the dramatic production crises that seemed his Sisyphean destiny to eternally confront.

The sold-out show was a five-hour music marathon, with an acoustic set from the Dead, then Jerry and the New Riders of the Purple Sage, and finally an all-electric set from the Dead. The concert finally ended early in the morning, and despite our exhaustion, we were eager to visit Jerry. Backstage was packed, but we managed to slip our way through to Jerry's dressing room, which was overflowing with friends and well-wishers. When Jerry saw David, he jumped up and motioned us over. "Hey, man! Great to see you," David cried, giving his old buddy a hug.

"Yeah man, same here!" Jerry exclaimed.

"Jerry, Richard was my agent with Earth Opera," David said, nodding in my direction.

"All right!" Jerry said, extending his hand.

"Yeah, and before that he was Liberace's agent." We all shared a laugh over that one.

"Far out!" Jerry intoned. "He must have been quite a trip!"

Jerry listened intently as I told the story of how Liberace had gotten me into the music business. Jerry had an affable demeanor, and I felt relaxed. The conversation shifted to music and the Dead's new album. We told him how much we liked *Workingman's Dead*, but Jerry was more interested in talking about the new songs he was working on with Robert Hunter for *American Beauty*. (A few months later, Jerry asked David to play on that album.)

As the dressing room emptied, Jerry opened up his silver cigarette case filled with prerolled joints, lit one up, and started talking nonstop. He was so into what he was saying that he'd forget to pass the joint. David would jokingly chide, "Hey, Jerry, you ever gonna pass that thing?" The three of us raved about everything— Altamont, the Dead bust in New Orleans, and politics. We finally got around to telling Jerry about Hieronymusic, the Rowan Brothers, how disheartening it was that they'd been rejected by several record companies, and the frustrations we were having trying to launch them. "Hey, you guys should move your trip to the Bay Area. You can play in a hundred clubs. The scene is much more relaxed out there. I'll put in a good word for you!"

David and I looked at each other. Wow! Once again, life had abruptly transformed from the bleak and disconsolate to the bright and promising. As we left the Fillmore early that morning, we had made our decision. We were definitely in "A California state of mind"!

# PART TWO:

## STINSON BEACH, CALIFORNIA

*David Grisman, the Rowan Brothers,
Garcia-Saunders, and Old and in the Way*

# CHAPTER 14

## HALCYON DAYS

It was a hell of a transition from the frantic, humid, and ultra-urban streets of New York City to the laid-back, rolling dunes of the blue Pacific, but David and I had no second thoughts about heeding Jerry's advice and relocating to California. The adventuresome move continued to take shape under the auspices of good luck and good friends.

We started transferring our business operations from gritty New York to the idyllic San Francisco Bay Area in late summer, 1970. In September, I flew out to California ahead of everyone else to find suitable housing for the Hieronymusic entourage. Marty Balin had invited me to crash with him while I got things set up, so I headed out to Marin County. He had a rustic home in Mill Valley bursting with character, full of books and testaments to his many interests. The mind-blowing mélange of his eclectic, artistic creativity made it impossible not to be inspired around Marty.

Mill Valley was tucked into the leafy woods at the base of Mount Tamalpais, a peak whose soaring beauty was symbolic of upscale, bucolic Marin County. A community of hippies and rock-tolerant, wealthy liberals supported this colorful little enclave, which seemed park-like with its quaint boutiques framing the small village green. It was a heavenly place with a Shangri-La setting, and la crème de la crème of the Bay Area's celebrity musicians nested there in the seclusion of their redwood homes.

Marty was a thoughtful, welcoming friend and host. He went out of his way to acquaint me with the area's beautiful places and to introduce me to relevant industry contacts. Shortly after I arrived, he invited me to several recording sessions for Paul Kantner's Blows Against the Empire album, to which members of Jefferson Airplane as well as David Crosby and Jerry Garcia were contributing. Watching and listening to how technology and music were fused in the production of an album was a fascinating first for me.

The experience went hand in hand with another first, Merck pharmaceutical cocaine, the session's buffet drug. The fluffy white tincture was situated on the recording console in a brown bottle with a skull and crossbones label. That label signaled its toxic potential to the dentists who used it as a topical anesthesia—and its lethal appeal to recreational users. Merck's coke was not an organic compound but a synthetically manufactured drug that packed an insidious punch. Musicians, engineers, and guests freely and openly indulged, assuring me that I had definitely landed in California, not Kansas.

## A Dwelling on the Edge of the Western World

Leaving the shirelike environs of Mill Valley and winding westward through the mountains, the ribbon of Highway 1 glides down along the coastal cliffs into a postcard stretch of custom homes and small businesses that adorn an undulating line of white Pacific beaches. This paradise was Stinson Beach.

With the help of a realtor Marty knew, I found the perfect oceanfront house for the Hieronymusic encampment. It was spacious and beautifully designed, with an outbuilding that could serve as a perfect rehearsal hall. The area was a relatively isolated, small community populated by mostly seasonal renters. I signed a one-year lease with the owner, who had no idea that a gypsy band was about to settle into his house along this enchanting border of earth and sea.

I called David in New York to let him know I'd found a place and told him I'd seen Jerry at the Kantner sessions. A few days later, David arrived from the East Coast with the Rowan brothers, girlfriends, and dogs. We all settled in, and David and I devised a team game plan. He was going to choose and hone the tunes and put together a couple of set lists; I was going to land some club gigs to get them some exposure, stir up some excitement, and create a local following. We hoped to elicit the interest of the big record companies and create a bidding war for contracts. David began in earnest, setting up the rehearsal hall-recording studio in the garage and putting a Rowan Brothers show together while I tended to the business details. The Rowans continued to write songs and refine their performance skills.

## Credit Card Hippies

We were living an idyllic lifestyle. We continued our healthy food regime, played music for entertainment, practiced yoga, used the beach for exercise, grew our own pot, and maxed out our credit cards. Everyone was following his dreams, but no one had a paying job. We were living on both the geographical edge of the Western world and the financial edge of our resources. Every paradise has a snake—ours was the bill collector—but we were happy, high, healthy, and hopeful.

As it turned out, not everyone in Stinson loved having a commune of long-haired, dope-smoking, guitar-playing, good-for-nothing hippies in the neighborhood. One morning the phone rang, and to our surprise an unknown caller said, "Hello, this is a mission of mercy. Colonel White knows about your pot growing and has notified the sheriff." Colonel White was the ex-military fire chief who patrolled the beach in his Jeep, on the watch for fire hazards, burglars, Cold War spies, and any threats to the American Way of Life. We figured that a local electrician who'd been on the property to do repairs had tipped him off about our four-flowerpot marijuana operation. When the sheriff and the colonel arrived, the Great Stinson Beach Dope Raid failed to turn up any evidence of degenerate, criminal activity thanks to the anonymous tip. We were extremely grateful to our anonymous caller.

## Look Who's Coming to Dinner

"You know who's living in Stinson Beach? Jerry Garcia," David said one afternoon, returning from a munchies-run to town. "He lives up the hill on a dead-end road. We had a nice rap. He just signed a contract with Warner Brothers to record a solo record and used his advance for the down payment on the house. He said to come on up and play some music."

"Let's do it," I said.

It was fortuitous that we should all end up in the same little town, just a few short months after Jerry had encouraged us to move west. In the ensuing weeks and months, Grisman, the Rowans, and I spent a good bit of time visiting Jerry and Mountain Girl, his girlfriend since the mid-sixties. Their house was modest and located in a private cul-de-sac with a spectacular view of the coast.

Invariably, Jerry would carefully select premium cannabis buds from his extensive pot pantry and twist up joints for the long hours of music and conversation that followed. During our visits, Jerry often played tapes of recording sessions he'd made the night before, interspersed with everything from the Swan Silvertones to the Stanley Brothers. Jerry had taken up the pedal steel guitar and was playing and recording with the New Riders of the Purple Sage. He had an eclectic taste in music, but most of the time we listened to legendary bluegrass tunes, the genre in which he and David shared a proclivity. One night after listening to a Homer and Jethro song, Jerry said, "I gotta get back to practicing the banjo."

"Yeah, man!" David was encouraging. "I'm ready to play. Just say the word." Moments like these laid the groundwork for Old and in the Way, the musical group they formed a couple years later.

Jerry loved the Rowan Brothers' songs, did all he could to help launch their career, and played pedal steel guitar with them on their album. We all profited personally and professionally during this creative period of reciprocal interchange in Stinson Beach.

## The Big Break and the Breakup

David and I took the Rowan Brothers to LA, where I had arranged for them to audition for David Geffen and Clive Davis—two of the most important figures in the record business. I had known David Geffen, the president and owner of Asylum Records, from my days in New York when we were both agents vying for talent. Clive was president of Columbia Records, *the* premier record label in the industry.

Just as we'd hoped and planned, both Asylum and Columbia liked what they heard and began competing to sign the brothers.

Clive offered us a two-year, three-record contract rather than the usual deal of one year with four one-year options, plus a fifty-thousand dollar signing bonus. And he agreed to let Grisman produce the album rather than insisting on a renowned producer. The combination sealed the deal for us, and we went with Columbia. At the time, it was the biggest deal for a new artist in the history of the record company. Years later, when their contract with Columbia terminated, the Rowan Brothers went on to record for Asylum Records.

Life began to change and accelerate rapidly when we received the large cash advance and sizeable budget to produce the record. The Rowans did a series of LA gigs to generate attention, David brought in engineers and musicians for studio work, and a billboard appeared on Sunset Strip that read: "The Rowan Brothers, one of the most important new sounds since The Beatles"—Jerry Garcia.

The big break had arrived, but it came with some unforeseen consequences. Columbia had invested heavily and the company's executives determined how the Rowans would be promoted. David and I felt that they should be promoted as a duo with an emphasis on singles and showcased in teen-oriented magazines and in small clubs. The suits felt that they should perform in large, cavernous arenas before screaming rock fans and insisted on the traditional rock band formula: release the album and support it with a tour.

At the insistence of Columbia Records, the Rowans went on tour as the opening act for the Grateful Dead. With their boyish charms, delicate Simon and Garfunkel–Everly Brothers harmonies, and catchy commercial songs, the Rowans could not have been more dissimilar to the Grateful Dead. The Dead's audience wanted to like them because Jerry had said they were great, but the match was all wrong.

The Rowan Brothers' record came out with mostly good reviews without a hit single; album sales faded and failed to meet Columbia Records' expectations. Columbia had committed to another two records, but it soon became evident that without a hit record and high-paying gigs, our collective venture was unsustainable and we had to go our separate ways. We had pooled our efforts and given the launch of the Rowan Brothers our best shot, but it just wasn't to be. We had all been on such a high for a year with great expectations for the success of the album that its failure, and the subsequent dissolution of the enterprise in mid-1972, was disappointing and deflating beyond belief.

The dreams of Hieronymusic lay buried somewhere beneath the white sands of Stinson Beach.

## Cliffhanger

I was distraught and worried about what I would do for work. Unlike David, I wasn't a musician and didn't have a career in music. I was back to thinking about my New York experience in the business and how I would never again wade in those shark-infested waters. When David and I formed our partnership, it was different than my work as an agent at APA—we were friends working together toward a common goal in a comfortable, open, and friendly environment. At APA, I was negotiating and dealing with unsavory, disreputable managers and promoters. I was once again at a career impasse, not knowing which way to turn.

# CHAPTER 15

# SOMETIMES THE LIGHT'S ALL SHINING ON ME

"Hey man, I gotta lot goin' on in my life besides the Dead. Wanna help me out? You know, coordinate stuff, set up gigs, organize session work. . ."

"Are you kidding? Shit yeah! Far out!" I answered in a nanosecond, interrupting Jerry before he finished his list. "Cool man!" Jerry smiled and started telling me about his projects outside the Dead. That was my formal contract to work for Jerry Garcia. With Jerry, all you needed was mutual understanding. We reached that understanding at his home in Stinson Beach in 1972, shortly after the dissolution of Hieronymusic. Our agreement couldn't have come at a better time because I was quickly using up my resources. The money Jerry offered was modest, but I was happy to have something coming in and the boost to my spirits was enormous.

Working with Jerry was an honor and a pleasure. He had already become a legend and was in constant demand. I never found him to be egotistical, difficult, or manipulative and was not surprised to learn that he was truly beloved by his associates and friends. As I got to know him better in the eight years that followed, my respect for him continued to grow and we became close friends. He was not a saint by any means, and he had a well-known weakness for drugs, but friends are friends and my friend Jerry had a lot of stuff going on that needed organizing.

His central role was with the Dead, but he was thoroughly enjoying his other roles in a bunch of satellite projects as well—playing pedal steel guitar and recording with the New Riders of the Purple Sage, and serving as a musical consultant on albums for groups such as Crosby, Stills, and Nash and Jefferson Airplane. Jefferson Airplane credited him as "spiritual advisor" on their breakout album, *Surrealistic Pillow.* Around the same time, he started playing gigs with jazz-oriented musicians, which evolved into the Garcia-Saunders Band. Whether it was rock, jazz, or bluegrass, music was a source of wonder and fascination to Jerry. His life was music, and the more varied and challenging it was, the more engaged he became. Practicing and performing took all his time and energy, and he really did need a manager to look after the practical details and the business end of his affairs.

I had learned from my years in the music business what a good manager is and does. Loving and respecting the artist is a must and creating an environment that allows the artist the freedom to go wherever the muse takes him is just as important as lending guidance, support, and advice when needed—and knowing when it's not. For the manager-artist relationship to be successful, the artist must not only be kept up-to-date on all career issues and decisions but also share in the decision-making.

My manager-artist relationship with Jerry was a natural from the beginning. We were a great team and successfully supported and helped each other navigate through a business known for its volatilities and estrangements.

## Keystone Cops and Comics

He was about six foot five and at least two hundred twenty-five pounds, had bulging biceps protruding from his leather vest, and was giving me the stank eye. I felt like I had just stepped between a pit bull and his bone when Jerry looked up from noodling on his guitar and said, "Steve, that's Richard, he's cool."

"He don't look cool," Steve sneered.

Jerry kept playing scales, knowing that Steve Parish was initiating me into the backstage club at Keystone Berkeley. Big Steve was chief roadie. He humped Jerry's amps and equipment to all the gigs but was first and foremost Jerry's protector. Steve was also part of the Grateful Dead crew, a fiercely tight and highly paid clan. They traveled first class, had the best drugs, and were intimidating. Over time, Steve and I became good friends, but I had to endure the usual hazing before being accepted.

At the Keystone for the first time, I had found my way to the dressing room, where the musicians and the crews hung out and smoked weed before the show. Big Steve and another roadie, Kidd Candelario, were blowing a joint and Jerry was practicing when a congenial-looking, dark-haired guy walked in.

Steve yelled, "Hey, Freddie, wadda ya want? We told you to stay outta here. We're gettin' high for the show, man." Freddie Herrera had heard it all before, and it didn't faze him. He was the club owner and operator and part of the inner circle.

"Hey, Freddie, this here's Richard," Jerry announced. "He's going to be handling the money and bookings for us from now on." Freddie nodded.

Steve muttered, "Bean counter."

As Merl Saunders, Jerry's talented keyboard partner, entered the dressing room, Freddie said, "It's starting to fill up out there. You guys go on in about an hour. Let me know if you need anything."

"I could use a beer!" Steve said.

"You could use a bath!" Freddie shot back as he exited, giving me a nod to follow him.

"Man!" I said smiling and shaking my head from side to side. "Are they always like that?"

"Only if they like you," Freddy said. "Otherwise, they can be real assholes."

We laughed. "Come on up to my office. I'll give you the rundown."

The Keystone was a home for local bands looking for exposure and small change. It was a small, bare club—a hundred by seventy-five feet at most, with high ceilings, an elevated stage, and a few scattered tables. The knee-high benches along the walls to the left and right of stage were always packed with fans, who could perch for a better view of the stage over the heads of the dancers. Freddie's office was upstairs, with a window that looked out onto the stage and the crowd below. It was the management's version of the musicians' backstage area, and something about it was comfortable and welcoming.

"Just push that shit on the floor," Freddie said, motioning to a chair piled high with stuff. "I sell beer by the pitcher and popcorn by the bag," he went on to explain. "I make most of my money from beer sales, and pay the musicians in cash from the door receipts.

Depending on the amount we'd take in, I'd allocate a few hundred dollars to Steve, Kidd, and myself, another hundred or so to our office expenses, and the rest to the musicians. Even though Jerry was the draw, he always insisted that all the musicians be paid equal amounts.

The band hit the stage around ten o'clock, and I left Freddie's office to listen to music. I think the club's legal max capacity was two hundred fifty, but the place was packed. I'd heard that on Garcia-Saunders weekends, Freddie packed in as many as five hundred, and it must have been one of those nights. I'd never heard the band with Bill Vitt on drums and John Kahn on bass, and they blew me away. They ripped through an amazing range of musical styles—Dylan covers, R&B, blues, reggae, and rock—and closed with Junior Parker's "Mystery Train" and a driving guitar solo by Jerry that brought down the house. I was amazed at how vocally emotive and animated Jerry was, much more so than when I'd seen him with the Dead.

It was an exciting and productive period of varied musical activity in Jerry's life, and it was my pleasure to be around him and hear him perform in so many genres. He was relaxed and free of his rock star identity when he played outside the big rock venues for his adoring fans. When Jerry later played in Old and in the Way with Vassar Clements, Peter Rowan, John Kahn, and David Grisman, the bluegrass aficionados had no idea who the bearded banjo player was. Jerry loved just being another musician and not a recognized celebrity. At one point, he summed up his feelings in *Melody Maker*, "The most rewarding experience for me these days is to play in bars and not be Jerry Garcia of the Grateful Dead. I enjoy playing to fifty people. The bigger the audience gets, the harder it is to be light and spontaneous."

## Family Feuds

Although these projects were great for Jerry, they didn't sit well with some of the other Grateful Dead members. The band was not yet making the big money that would come later. There were rumblings in the Dead community that Jerry's activities were a costly distraction, limiting the Dead's engagement schedule and their paychecks. Jerry always made the Dead his first priority, but his pure love of music transcended monetary considerations and he was seduced by the muse in all shapes and forms, which meant playing not only with the Grateful Dead. Jerry was above reproach, so as his manager, I became the brunt of all the resentment. For me, Jerry came first, and I found myself having to juggle feelings on both sides with a positive attitude, as diplomatically as possible. I had to deal with a complex web of relationships, both within and surrounding the band.

One character in the Dead community was Ron Rakow, a high-finance wheeler-dealer who convinced the band to form Grateful Dead Records in 1972. Rakow is a strange footnote in the history of the Dead. This slick and self-assured businessman, high-level Scientologist, and low-level hippie managed to ingratiate himself into the Dead community, where he concocted a number of weird and shady deals. One involved a sixteen-car fleet of British-made Ford Cortinas, which he leased at a bargain rate to members of the Dead family to get around Marin County. The cars, the subject of some hilarious stories, all ended up destroyed, broken, and abandoned in the hills and lagoons of Marin. Many of his schemes, wacky as they were, seemed harmless—until one day the band discovered that he was responsible for glaring irregularities in the Dead accounts. Confronted by Phil Lesh and others, his explanation was, "Go fuck yourselves!" He wrote himself a severance check for two hundred twenty-five thousand bucks and disappeared from the scene. Years later, his financial shenanigans finally caught up with him, and he spent five years behind bars.

Ron had always been friendly and generous to me because of my close association with Jerry, but I never trusted him. I could recognize a shark after my New York experiences, even one posing as a hippie entrepreneur. I made a point of maintaining a good distance from Ron and not getting involved with him or any of his schemes. Ironically, I went through a strange spell with some of the band members and crew, who mistakenly thought Ron and I were in cahoots simply because we both lived in Stinson Beach and shared a friendship with Jerry. I heard rumors that we were referred to as the "Stinson Beach Mafia," the nefarious outsiders who were trying to take over the Dead. It was my first direct introduction to the nasty business of Dead family rumors, jealousies, and suspicions. My friendship with Jerry kept me from walking away.

## A Day in the Life

Shortly after I started working for Jerry, it was obvious we needed a place to conduct business. I rented a one-room office in Mill Valley, halfway between our homes in Stinson Beach and the Grateful Dead office in San Rafael. We hired Sue Stephens, my devoted assistant from the Rowan Brothers days, picked up some furniture, installed phones, bought a movie projector, and put together a small sound system. What the office lacked in designer décor, it made up for in relaxed and easygoing ambiance.

On typical mornings, Jerry walked in around nine o'clock, slapped his briefcase down on the desk, grabbed a big mug of coffee, pulled up a chair, laid out a couple of lines, lit a joint, and began the day. Mornings were spent tending to business, watching movies on reels I'd rented from LA, or jawing with anyone who popped into the office. Jerry's Bay Area friends and musicians dropped by from time to time with stories and news from the odd collection of places and people that made up Jerry's world. In those days, Jerry was vibrant and active. I treasured our friendship, which was deep and meaningful. The bond we established during those times made it all the more painful for me to see him, long after our days together, slide into addiction and self-isolation.

## Music, Magic, and the Occult

Music is a kind of magic that casts a spell of enchantment. To be deeply moved or transported by music is to experience its ineffable power. Neurochemistry and physics analyze this phenomenon, but science cannot explain or express the spirit of a song. Musicians are intuitive magicians, and no musician was more aware or immersed in this mystery than Jerry.

In the 60s and 70s, an occult revival coincided with the hippie movement, the rise of rock, and experimentation with drugs. Jerry, Phil Lesh, Marty Balin, and I (as well as many others) were fascinated with the esoteric. We all felt that drugs, music, and art could access or mimic dimensions of consciousness.

Those ideas were referred to in many musical, lyrical, and artistic themes explored by the Dead and Jefferson Airplane. For instance, the graphic art associated with the Dead used bold, visual metaphors in reverence to that mystery and magic. The shared interest for the arcane inspired both art and song and wove the ties of friendship.

## Spud, Dawg, Red, Zippy, Clem, Mule, and Bear

Memory is a maze with strange and unexpected connections, and when I recall those journeys into altered states, one character whose contributions to both the mystical and the musical must be mentioned—Owsley "Bear" Stanley.

When I met him, he was already a legend from his days with Ken Kesey and the Merry Pranksters, from the acid trip concerts, and from his notorious busts and freak-outs. He was a major presence in the Dead community, devoted to the band, and revered for his innovative sound engineering and LSD expertise. He was a unique and remarkable man—an important and influential music archivist, recorder, and seeker—whose LSD exploits were chronicled by Tom Wolfe in his book *The Electric Kool-Aid Acid Test.*

When I was Jerry's manager in the early seventies, Jerry, David Grisman, and Peter Rowan started hanging out at Jerry's house in Stinson Beach to play bluegrass and traditional acoustic music for their own enjoyment. Jerry played his old Weymann five-string banjo and the three jammed out archival bluegrass tunes. I was never a big bluegrass music fan, but there in Jerry's living room, I soon found myself sharing the joy these three guys were having playing tunes from their musical roots and became transfixed by the sound I was hearing. They had left behind this music to pursue other musical goals, and now they were playing it again. They were enjoying every moment, and their exuberance was infectious.

Jerry, David, and Peter decided to form a band, and Jerry recruited his friend, the Garcia-Saunders bassist John Kahn, to join on upright acoustic bass. This exciting project for old friends became Old and in the Way. I accepted their offer to manage the band's affairs, and they were off and running. Rehearsals started, songs were chosen, and after just a few living room rehearsals, Garcia, always more eager to perform than rehearse, suggested, "Hey, man. This is fun! We should play in a few bars and see where it takes us."

David invited Richard Greene to play fiddle; when he couldn't make it, John Hartford sat in. The first couple of gigs were small, loose, informal affairs in Stinson Beach that were quickly followed by a dozen performances in Bay Area clubs. I put forward the idea that they play some gigs on the East Coast. The band was without a permanent fiddle player, so David suggested that they try to get Vassar Clements. We contacted Vassar in Nashville, and in a matter of days, he arrived at the first gig in Boston and proceeded to blow everybody's socks off. Vassar, like Peter, was a veteran of Bill Monroe's band and was regarded by many as the greatest fiddler alive. Jerry, of course, had an enormous fan base.

Old and in the Way was a band of unique revelers, on stage and off, who energized each other. John had a brilliant dry wit and played an omnipresent bass; Peter's singing and songwriting were brilliant; David's quest for perfection on the mandolin was unwavering; Vassar, with his pipe clenched tightly between his teeth, played faultlessly; and Jerry, with his huge heart, was determined to conquer the banjo. Delighted by the challenge of David's and Vassar's licks, Jerry held his own and made the banjo his constant companion.

Everyone had nicknames. Peter was Red because he'd written "Panama Red." Grisman dubbed Garcia, Spud, and Garcia, in turn, named David, Dawg. Vassar was Clem, and Kahn was Mule. Kahn gave me the name Zippy because I was always moving quickly and am a high-energy kinda guy. The band was a lot of fun for me: I loved the music, the guys were a hoot to be around, and there were no pain-in-the-ass technical complications because the band had no road crew or bulky equipment.

One unexpected presence, however, was the Grateful Dead soundman Owsley "Bear" Stanley. He took it upon himself to turn up at the band's gigs just before showtime with his mikes and recording gear. He'd fiddle endlessly with the equipment until everything was precisely adjusted, which often caused long performance delays. The wait drove the punctual Jerry crazy. He would pace and silently seethe backstage until the signal was given that they were set to go. In the end, though, we have Owsley to thank for three albums of great music from a band that came and went all too soon. The group disbanded within a year and the members returned to their own projects, leaving a legacy that defied convention and forever changed our world—just like our late, good friend and self-described Acid King, Bear Owsley.

Old and in the Way interpreted music from a variety of sources, including rock and blues, and added original songs such as Peter's famous "Panama Red." Their first album went on to become the best-selling bluegrass record at the time, introducing the genre to many and creating a new group of fans.

# PART THREE:

# THE GRATEFUL DEAD

*Politics, Grateful Dead Movie, Garcia Bands, Egypt, Saturday Night Live, Alaska, and Radio City Music Hall*

# CHAPTER 16

## COMPLIMENTS AND CHANGES

In September 1973, Ron Rakow needed new product for Round Records—the subsidiary of Grateful Dead Records owned by Garcia and Rakow—and he was on Jerry's case to make another album.

Jerry was into doing something completely different for his second solo venture. He turned to his good friend John Kahn, the bass player from Old and in the Way and the Garcia-Saunders Band, and asked him to produce the record. John was also a close friend of mine, and he asked me to be the production coordinator. John had been a music mentor for me, expanding my musical knowledge and introducing me to a variety of genres from his vast collection. We shared musical interests, and he knew we could work well together. The new album would eventually be called *Compliments*, and I was thrilled and honored to be part of it.

Most of the recording took place in LA in late December 1973. John had top session musicians lay down the basic tracks first, and then he used Jerry as a vocalist and support player. The approach was to insert a dramatically different approach compared to how Jerry recorded with the Dead. John chose songs that not only fit Jerry's vocal range but also reflected their shared lyrical and musical tastes, including selections from Van Morrison, Dr. John, the Rolling Stones, Chuck Berry, Smokey Robinson, and Irving Berlin. In an interview about the sessions, Jerry said, "I went in there like a studio vocalist with the lyrics. Most of them I'd only heard once or twice before. It was one of the few times I didn't really go on a trip about the material. I let John select most all of it, but I made a few suggestions like . . . 'Russian Lullaby' was my idea."

The album and style were a huge departure for Jerry. Some of his Dead fans were disappointed, but sales were good and the critical response from reviewers was encouraging. For me, the fun of collaborating creatively with two close friends was a great learning experience in the art of record production, and working on *Compliments* remains one of the highlights of my career.

## Angel Archives

On a bright September day in 1973, had Liberty been a live lady instead of a statue in New York Harbor, she would have raised her eyebrows in disdain at the sight of "the wretched refuse" partying on the passing steamship. They were not the tired, the poor, or the huddled masses yearning to breathe free; they were the Hells Angels drinking beer, sucking nitrous oxide out of party balloons, and rollicking on the upper deck of the SS *Bay Belle*. Specifically, they were members of the New York City and Richmond chapter of the Hells Angels outlaw biker club and their friends. Resplendent in leathers and tattoos, they were rocking to the sounds of Bo Diddley as he belted out "Who Do You Love?"

The Angels had always treated me with respect and loyalty, but I also had seen them suddenly snap and get in your face, so I thought it best to pocket my camera after a few cautious snapshots and not invite trouble. I was attending the raucous affair, appropriately called "The Hells Angels Pirate's Ball," with Jerry, Merle Saunders, Bill Kreutzmann, and John Kahn. We were guests of the Angels. The

Angels and members of the Dead community had maintained a connection ever since the 1967 acid-soaked Human Be-In celebration in San Francisco's Golden Gate Park. As voluntary, self-appointed security that day, the Angels and the twenty-thousand-plus crowd of hippies, band members, and the curious had melded together in drug-happy harmony.

The Angels, however, were not just big, stoned puppy dogs. Their presence always had an edge of unpredictability, and they could turn violent on a moment's notice, as they did at Altamont during the Rolling Stones concert. Their involvement as self-appointed security had escalated out of control, causing numerous fights and one death. The peace-loving hippies and the combative bikers couldn't have been more opposite, but the two groups had developed a common tie based on their love of freedom, distrust of the establishment, and affinity for drugs.

Sandy Alexander, the president of the New York City chapter of the Angels, felt that the Dead-Angel connection was solid enough to ask Jerry and Ron Rakow for funds to complete a documentary film about the club that they were making with Leon Gast, the director. Sandy introduced Ron and Jerry to Leon, who showed them the footage he'd already shot. Jerry was enthusiastic about the film, and he and Ron ended up investing well over two hundred fifty thousand dollars towards its completion.

The film, *Hells Angels Forever*, was a long time in the making. It was not released until 1983, long after Leon's 1975 work with Jerry as co-director on the highly successful Dead docu-film, *The Grateful Dead Movie*, but long before Leon's 1997 film on Mohammed Ali, *When We Were Kings*, won an Oscar for best documentary. *Hells Angels Forever* came out to mixed reviews and faded into obscurity, which was a shame. Leon did a great job with the film, painting an accurate and fascinating picture of an American cultural phenomenon.

Jerry was intrigued with the larger-than-life Angels, and the first East Coast tour of the Garcia-Saunders Band just *happened* to coincide with the Pirate's Ball the Angels were having in New York. Jerry had agreed to perform as a favor to Sonny Barger, the president of the Oakland Angels chapter, who was in prison at the time on federal charges. The event, which was on a boat that chugged around the New York harbor, was a benefit to raise funds for Barger's defense. Barger's supporters claimed that his arrest was part of a systematic attempt by the U.S. government to dismantle the club—and Jerry, who had been set up for a bust himself in New Orleans, was sympathetic.

The Angels' temperaments were ramping up fast, in close correlation to the increase in the consumption of drugs and alcohol. We were suddenly more aware of our isolation and situation: We were partying on a boat in the middle of a harbor with the elite of the outlaw biker world. They were a fearsome group, intimidating not just in size, and we felt a growing apprehension as the action became more frenzied. Surrounded by a seemingly friendly pack of dogs but wary of their ferocious potential if paws got stepped on, we were treading carefully. We discreetly retreated to the ship's boiler room, which was serving as the makeshift backstage. It occurred to me that we were somewhat removed from the boisterous deck crowd above but now trapped in a confined space below, and that space shrank dramatically when Big Vinnie pushed his way into our midst.

Vinnie was huge—well over six feet tall and more than three hundred pounds, with a bearded pug face, massive arms, and a pumped-up chest protruding from his denim vest. He gesticulated wildly, flailing his spike-belted bulging arms perilously close to our faces. "I just come down here to see yous and make sure ya bein' treated right. Lemme know if ya have any problems need fixin'." Thoughts of having Big Vinnie hovering by my side when I had to deal with shady promoters distracted me, but I was interrupted from my daydream by Jerry's voice assuring Vinnie that there were no problems and we were delighted to be on board. Vinnie snorted his satisfaction and turned to leave. We were relieved to see him go.

Jerry watched Vinnie shuffling off. "Man, you gotta hand it to that guy! He's scary, but he's real."

"Yeah! Real scary!" I added.

Jerry smiled. "Yeah. He's just who he is." He believed that there was something uniquely American about the Angels—their toughness, independence, and directness. Jerry accepted people for who they were, on their terms, without judgment.

Years later, we heard that Big Vinnie ended up in prison for throwing a girl from a rooftop to her death. It was tragic news but not surprising.

The news brought back memories of the Pirate's Ball. We had lucked out and all had gone well for us, but the apprehensive feelings we'd felt on the boat came flooding back at the mention of Big Vinnie's name.

## Angel Dust Up

The Angels and the Dead's shared mutual respect was a comfort of sorts, but the Angels' involvement introduced a nerve-wracking, explosive potential for someone in my position. I respected Jerry's feelings about the Angels and his financial and social ties to the club, but dealing with them in concert situations was extremely difficult.

The Garcia Band ended up playing at another Pirate's Ball several years after our first experience, but for the most part I tried to shy away from Sandy Alexander's persistent attempts to promote the band. I had started working with John Scher and his company, Monarch Entertainment, for our East Coast shows, and I used our commitment to John when necessary as a reason for not being able to do shows outside the Monarch umbrella. It helped me fend off Sandy's requests but ended up unintentionally casting John as the bad guy, an undesirable role at best.

John was promoter in 1978 when the Dead did a Giant Stadium concert in East Rutherford City, the night before the band's Egypt tour. At the last minute, Sandy Alexander informed John that forty to fifty Angels would be attending the concert, and he wanted permission for them to park their bikes in the area beneath the stadium. This request was actually a favor by Angels' protocol, and when Angels asked for favors they expected favors to be given. John relayed the request to the Jersey Sports Exposition Authority but was emphatically denied. To appease Sandy, John offered to cordon off a section of the parking lot for the bikes, but Sandy was furious and threatened the now-terrified John. Shortly after their encounter, I got a call from Sandy demanding that I tell John to let the Angels park under the stadium or else. We appealed to the Sports Authority, who were growing increasingly nervous about the Angels, and they responded by getting the mayor of Jersey City to back them up on their denial. John, who was no longer sleeping at night, begged me and the band to do something—anything.

Jerry and I went down to the club headquarters at Seventy-seven East Third Street, the safest street in New York thanks to the Angels, who the local working-class residents regarded as guardians. Sandy greeted us with, "What the fuck's with this asshole Scher? Is he tryin' to mess with us?"

"Believe me, Sandy," I said with complete sincerity, "nobody's trying to mess with you!"

"We don't like it any better than you do," Jerry chimed in, "but we don't make the rules."

"Rules! What fuckin' rules, man?" "John tried his best. He . . ."

"Bullshit!" Sandy interrupted. "He's a fuckin' liar!" Jerry gave Sandy his best what-can-we-do? look.

Sandy liked Jerry and reached over and patted him on the shoulder. "Ya wanna know about rules, man? There's only one goddamn rule—ya take what ya want and fuck the rest."

"We're really sorry, Sandy," Jerry offered.

"Ah, don't worry 'bout it. We're gonna park underneath." Sandy shrugged. "No problem."

"But . . . but . . .," I stuttered.

"We talked to some guys we know and got the Jersey State Troopers to put pressure on the stadium dickheads. They changed their minds. Know what I mean? We're parkin' underneath."

Jerry and I exchanged looks of relief.

Sandy nodded at us. "That's how the fuckin' rules work!"

## Beatle Juiced and the Banality of Fame

"I want to jam with 'em. Get me a guitar louder than J.C.'s!" John Lennon told me.

"J.C.? You mean Jerry," I said, amused by my imagined image of Jesus in a band.

"I mean Jerry what's-his-name, in the black T-shirt," Lennon replied.

1974 was an odd and pivotal year, with a lot of disquiet. People were being challenged and pressured. The pendulum swing was reaching an apex, and the Piper was having a field day.

On the Fourth of July weekend, the Garcia-Saunders Band was playing in New York at the Bottom Line on West Fourth Street in Greenwich Village. The Dead had just finished an East Coast tour, and Jerry's *Compliments* album had been recently released. The owners of the Bottom Line had contacted me back in February, offering a four-show engagement for the Garcia-Saunders Band, and we'd accepted. I arranged for John Kahn and Merl to fly in, and John brought along his girlfriend at the time, Maria Muldaur, who was riding high on her hit single "Midnight at the Oasis." She sat in as a guest vocalist, and the group was hot. Word got out, and lines stretched around the block for every show. The Bottom Line was *the* happening place to be in the city, and all sorts of people were showing up.

John Lennon showed up backstage at the beginning of his eighteen-month "Lost Weekend" estrangement from Yoko, and he was shit-faced. After making his bizarre request for a guitar louder than Jerry's, he turned and left, leaving me thinking, "What the hell was that?" When Jerry took his backstage break, I relayed Lennon's desire to sit in with a louder guitar. "What the fuck!" Jerry snorted. Lennon returned and repeatedly kept calling Jerry "J.C." Fueled by alcohol and who knows what else, he was creeping me out with his uncool behavior. Jerry, however, simply ignored the drunk Beatle and kept his distance.

To me, John Lennon had always been a hero and an icon, and it was hard for me to see him stumbling around, a bad drunk, grappling with his demons in public. His music and his songs attested to another side of the man, and if he had shown up sober, his encounter with Jerry that evening could have evolved into something extraordinary. After the show, I asked Jerry, "What'd ya think about that?"

"About what?"

"Lennon! Don't you think that was weird?"

Jerry pulled out a joint, lit it, took a puff, and shrugged. "Yeah, no one ever took me for Jesus before."

## Dead Man Walking

"The people who lead bands from relative obscurity to mega popularity are not usually very nice people! Nowadays, managers are diplomats; in my day, they were aggressive bastards who got what they needed for their band come what may." That bit of wisdom is courtesy of Sam Cutler, former road manager for the Rolling Stones and the Grateful Dead's agent from 1972 to 1974.

He definitely knew how to be a bastard and how to get what was needed. He was ambitious and clever, and he had street smarts and a good business sense. Leveraging his imposing, tenacious personality, he soon became the controlling force of the Dead operation, which up to that time was organizationally loose and leaderless. Sam made some positive contributions to the Dead scene but overplayed his hand, exercised too much power, and played people against each other. He ultimately caused his own demise and was fired by the Dead in January 1974.

When I got a call from Jon McIntire, the Dead's manager, asking me to stop by his office, I wasn't sure what to expect. Jon stood out in sharp contrast to the scruffy casual types in the Dead community. He was tall, blonde, strikingly handsome, well dressed, educated, and gay. He was a chic and elegant anomaly in a crowd of denim, tie-dye, ponytails, and beards. I found Jon to be genuine, pleasant, courteous, and reasonable, and we got along well. I was anxious and puzzled about this special meeting and was surprised when he said, "Richard, Sam Cutler is no longer working for us. Would you like to book us?"

I was stunned. Be the agent for the Grateful Dead! I tried to appear casual. "Yeah," I said. "I heard Sam was let go. What happened?"

Jon sighed, and being his diplomatic self said, "He just wasn't working out for us. I prefer to leave it at that."

I didn't press the issue. "Well," I paused. "I certainly appreciate the offer. Let me think about it and talk to Jerry. It's a big responsibility. I'm not sure I can handle Sam's workload and look after Jerry's interests as well."

He smiled and held up his hand to dismiss my hedging. "Jerry knows about it," he said. "In fact, he suggested we offer you the job. He told us you used to book The Doors and Airplane when you worked in New York and have plenty of experience."

"Yeah, that's true but . . . .Well, thanks, Jon. It sounds like an exciting opportunity. Let me sleep on it, and I'll let you know tomorrow."

"My pleasure! Please do be sure to get back to me tomorrow. A lot is going on, and we need someone to begin planning our tour strategy right away."

"Sure enough," I responded.

It was nearly seven years since Danny Rifkin, the Dead's former manager, had turned down my offer to represent them while I was working for APA in New York. I had learned a lot and felt prepared to take on the challenge. I was thrilled to accept Jon's offer.

The initial changing of the guard, however, was not easy. I was not welcomed with open arms by those who had been Sam's friends, but Jerry had made the suggestion, Jon had made the offer, and I had accepted, for better or worse.

## Politics and the Wall of Sound

During the tumultuous year of 1974, I was hounded by two relentless headaches: band politics and the Wall of Sound. Sam Cutler's firing in January had created repercussions that were rippling through the Dead scene so fast they were impossible to keep up with. Members of the band, and especially the crew, resented Sam's termination, and rumors had started circulating that I had orchestrated his dismissal.

Sam had pampered the crew. He hung out with them on the road in their first-class accommodations and shared their expensive catered meals. He didn't have to deal with their drug-fueled, rowdy antics or their repeated confrontations and conflicts with promoters. He was, without question, their "one of the boys" buddy. I, on the other hand, was the businessman. Nobody likes the businessman— the one who deals with the financial realities, the "no" man—and my role with them was very different. Sam had always said yes, and I had to start saying no to make sure there were adequate funds to keep Grateful Dead Productions running smoothly. To some members of the band, but especially the crew, I was aloof and the bad guy. I tolerated their demands and bad attitudes as best I could, but their growing hostility was incredibly difficult for me to deal with.

My second headache was the Wall of Sound, a massive concert sound system designed by Owsley "Bear" Stanley. Despite sold-out shows and great sound quality, the system was financially unsustainable and a colossal mistake. The sound system took twelve hours or more to erect and almost as long to take down for every gig. In addition, a day off between gigs was required to allow the semitrucks to reach the next destination. The traveling troupe had grown to thirty or more, and the airfare, ground expenses, food, and lodging were astronomical, draining crippling amounts of cash from the band's earnings.

Tensions with the crew and the expense of the untenable sound system added to what was already an enormous booking challenge. I had scheduled a summer tour, thirty shows from May through the first week in August, but booking all those venues was grueling and draining. The tour was a grind—juggling personalities, altered and otherwise, was a relentless chore. I was exhausted, angry, and fed up with being grossly underpaid. At the end of the tour, I met Jon McIntire in New York and was finally able to vent my frustrations.

"I've had years of experience in this business. This setup is for shit! I know my worth, and I'm not going to work for grunt wages any longer. The goddamn crew guys make as much as me!" Jon was surprised by my outburst but supportive. I felt bad unloading on him, but I was happy to get my grievances off my chest. Jon promised he'd do what he could, but I knew his position wasn't an easy one either and that he was not popular with many of the new crew members. Their macho mentality was overwhelming the band's former hippie aesthetic.

Cocaine was changing everything. Of all the drugs I'd encountered on the scene, cocaine changed people's personalities the most and tended to fuel their egos and make them irrational. On pot or hash, people were happy, laid back, and nonconfrontational. On mushrooms, people were mellow and introspective. On acid, people were enlightened. Alcohol never improved anyone. Downers slowed people down. Speed gave people a crazy edge but not necessarily a nasty one.

The original choices on the Dead scene were typically pot, hash, mushrooms, and acid. The prospect of cocaine's widespread use was ominous.

# CHAPTER 17

## MADNESS AND MOVIES

"I quit!" Danny Rifkin announced. Everyone was back in California after the East Coast summer tour, and we were sitting at a band meeting at the Dead's office in San Rafael. Danny was a former Grateful Dead manager who had worked as a crew member on the just completed tour. "It's just no fun anymore," he said in a kind of deflated, matter-of-fact way.

No kidding. I had my own reasons for being displeased that were no secret, but Danny was speaking more for those in the Dead family who were unhappy and finding it increasingly difficult to deal with the escalating cocaine use and the presence of the "neo-cocaine cowboys," as John Barlow, the lyricist, called them. Most of the cowboys were recent additions to the road crew. The labor involved in transporting and setting up the Wall of Sound demanded muscle, and these guys were big, burly characters with surly attitudes and a taste for toot. They were riding high on coke, inflated salaries, and pumped-up egos. Dealing with them was a pain in the ass, and their salaries were sucking a small fortune out of Grateful Dead Productions.

In the fall of 1974, the band made the unwise decision to do a European tour. Labor and drug issues were mounting and should have been dealt with, but Rock Scully, who at this point was the band's publicist, wanted to drum up business for Tom Salter, an inexperienced promoter. Tom, who was flush in both drugs and money, was more of a rich groupie than a promoter. Rock worked hard to rally the band to tour, and they finally agreed to do a few dates abroad that September.

The tour had disaster written all over it. I was suspicious and fought against engaging with anyone but a reputable promoter with a bona fide business and an industry reputation to uphold. My admonition fell on deaf ears. In the end, I chose not to challenge Scully and bowed out completely. Jon McIntire was a little uneasy about the situation, knowing my reservations and having his own, but he was supportive of my decision. He suggested that I might like to accompany the band on the tour as a guest, at my own expense. The idea of being there in a nonworking capacity intrigued me, and I took him up on his offer. I loved Europe and was looking forward to being free of any band-related responsibilities.

## Burned Out from Exhaustion, Blown Out on the Trail

I arrived in London just in time to attend a band meeting before the first gig of the tour. The band and crew had already been doing a lot of nonstop, hard partying and were burned out. It was hard to ignore how out of control the situation had become.

Rex Jackson, a longtime and respected crew member, came down hard on the group, railing about the cocaine madness and challenging the group to toss their drug stashes and get it the fuck together. Bob Weir backed Rex, and others voiced concern. No one disagreed, but everyone in that room who had gotten into the stuff knew it had a stranglehold on them. Intentions were good, but I questioned how many stashes would get tossed after the meeting.

Even with the best intentions, I didn't think people could give it up just like that. In the end, usage just became more secretive.

The night of the first concert, I noticed a bunch of people bypassing the ticket line and heading down the alley beside the concert hall. Following them, I ended up at the back door, standing in front of a big guy in a security jacket.

"What's the deal?" I asked.

"You wanna get in cheap, luv?" He answered. "Just give me a couple of quid 'n' slide in!"

"What?"

"Are ya daft? Pay up or move on! You're holdin' up the bloody queue!"

Incredible! The venue's security guy was letting people in on the sly, undercutting ticket sales and pocketing money that should have been ours.

"Hey man, you can't do that!" I snapped back.

He pushed me off to the side with an angry glare, "Piss off, ya wanker."

I shot back up the alley and into the hall, searching for Rock. I finally located him backstage, hanging out with some crew guys, kicking back a rum and coke. "Rock, the security guys are ripping us off at the back door. Do you know about it?" I seemed more concerned about it than he did.

"Yeah, yeah, I told Tom. He's taking care of it. Want a snort?"

Everybody was high and having a good time, and no one seemed to care about what was going on. The London shows were a disaster. The crooked security continued to work the back door, and Tom, after proving he was a flakey promoter, tried to cop out on the contract.

The show moved on to Munich, where the partying continued out of control. Late one night after a show, Jon McIntire was startled and awakened in his hotel room by a loud and boisterous Bill Kreutzmann, the Dead's drummer. He demanded that Jon resign as manager. Bill considered Jon an effete intellectual and had never liked him.

All it took to send Kreutzmann over the edge were the disinhibiting effects of drugs, alcohol, and some trivial nonsense. As Bill was exiting the stage after the show, Jon hadn't seen him coming and had inadvertently bumped him—at least, that was as much of the story as anybody heard. The incident had obviously been eating away at Bill, and he was angry. Jon was a gentle guy, not cut out for that stuff, and he was deeply alarmed and shaken.

News of what had happened reached me the next morning. I checked in on Jon and suggested that we talk to Jerry. As Jon described the ordeal, Jerry just kept shaking his head sympathetically. "Man, I'd hate to see you go, but I wouldn't blame you one bit if you've had enough. I think if I were in your shoes, I'd probably just say fuck the Grateful Dead and do the same thing." Jon ended up resigning, not just because of Bill, although that certainly was part of it. Like Danny Rifkin, Jon decided it was just time to move on.

I left the tour with Jon. I'd had enough, too, but assured Jerry before leaving that I was still into handling his non-Dead affairs. Jon and I stopped off in France for a few days on our way back to California, and the Dead tour continued its death march across Europe, plagued by canceled shows, inept promoters, and a host of self-inflicted disasters. Back home, I busied myself with Jerry's projects and waited to see what would happen.

The ill-fated tour finally ended and everyone limped home. The general consensus was that many of the bad decisions and much of the unruly behavior were rooted in cocaine abuse. Grass and other "gateway-to-consciousness" entheogens were an integral part of the Dead culture's early years. The switch to high-grade cocaine may have been perpetuated by its ready availability or the need to ease the rigors of demanding tour schedules. Whatever the case, it exacted a heavy toll on the band and everyone involved with them. What had once been a mellow scene had imploded.

## Getting It Together

Days after the band returned from Europe, Bob Weir stopped by my Mill Valley office and wanted to know if I'd consider managing Grateful Dead Productions.

I had been in New York City from 1965 to 1970, so I didn't share the bonding with the band that others had in the early days of the Dead. Partly because of that, I seemed an odd match for the band in the beginning. While they were dropping acid, I was honing my skills in New York as an agent. The Dead, for all their proclamations of artistic freedom and creative indulgence, needed someone who could run the business end of things. I was a fiscal conservative and a social radical. During the 1974 summer tour that I'd booked for them, my agent's training and expertise had served them well, and they understood my value to their organization. Now I had to ask myself whether I wanted to manage Grateful Dead Productions, with all that had gone down.

I was thinking hard and long about the job offer and was invited to discuss it at a band meeting at the end of September. I knew what had gone on with some of their managers—deceit, disloyalty, embezzlement, and just plain misunderstandings—and I wanted to establish a setup that put us all at ease. I had decided I would take the job only under two conditions: one, my earnings would not exceed those of any single band member, hoping that would invite and assure financial transparency, and two, I'd work in my Mill Valley office and continue my independent work with Jerry. They agreed, and I accepted the job.

That October, I booked the band for five shows in San Francisco at Winterland. The band, no longer able to ignore everything that had happened on the European tour, unanimously voted to take a long overdue, indefinite hiatus after the shows.

No one was sure what might happen after the break, including never playing together again as a band. With that possibility looming, they decided they wanted to film the shows for themselves, the fans, and the Grateful Dead archives.

## Rockin' the Big Screen

Jerry asked Leon Gast to direct the project, and he and his crew of nine cameramen were at Winterland all five nights to shoot the shows and a bunch of interviews.

The documentary film had been financed before I became manager of Grateful Dead Productions, and my initial involvement with it was minimal. The movie turned out to be a bear, taking two and a half years to reach theaters. Jerry was the film's editorial director, and he put in endless hours and energy editing the film and soundtrack. He brought in Gary Gutierrez and his San Francisco special effects company, Colossal, to do an amazing animated opening sequence, and the project inched along. At times, the process seemed endless, and even Jerry wondered if it would ever get done.

Expenses piled up and the film's budget ballooned from one hundred twenty-five thousand dollars to six hundred thousand. The money that had been allotted originally had been spent, and the project was in the hole. With Rakow gone, I became the movie's "clean up the mess" de facto executive producer and was faced with having to find forty thousand dollars to pay for the final prints and get the film into theaters.

I looked around desperately for an angel to save the project, but they were conspicuously absent in the music biz. I had to go to the other end of the spectrum and ask that ole "friend of the devil" Bill Graham for the funds. I hated having to compromise our position by sucking up to a promoter. Worse yet, I hated having to give Bill a lien on our concert money and a you-owe-me-one edge in negotiations. He loved the Dead, and although he had been annoyed with the disruptions created by the filming during those five nights at Winterland, he coughed up the forty thousand dollars to finish the project.

The final step was distribution. I brainstormed with Garcia and John Scher, and we decided not to do the traditional distribution deal but to rent theaters in the most popular Dead cities, install the best sound systems, enlist local rock impresarios, and promote the film like a live concert.

The *Grateful Dead Movie* was one of the first rock band concerts captured on film. It premiered at the prestigious, deluxe single-screen Ziegfeld Theater in New York on June 1, 1977, to a sold-out house of adoring fans. It was a major event for Deadheads, a chance to see their idols perform on a big screen with concert-quality sound and exclusive interviews. It may not be the best rock band movie ever made, but it is a damn good one and is now a Deadhead classic.

## High Notes

Jerry's goal had been to make a film that would capture a moment in the band's history for posterity, and he was pleased with the results. The band *did* get back together after a year and a half hiatus, but to this day, old fans and fans born too late to see the Grateful Dead live at the peak of their career can now go to a 1974 Grateful Dead concert —even if it's only on a DVD.

# CHAPTER 18

## JAMMIN' WITH JERRY

Jerry's bands had various incarnations, but they all shared John Kahn's involvement as musical director. Jerry loved those bands and loved playing in them. He reserved his energies as a songwriter and an arranger for the Grateful Dead, but playing in other bands gave him the opportunity to interact with a variety of talented artists other than the Dead members, and he enjoyed being a carefree musician without the commander-in-chief responsibilities that were his when he played with the Dead.

When the Dead went on hiatus in the fall of 1974, the Garcia-Saunders Band played sixty gigs in a ninety-day stretch, closing out the year. In early 1975, the band changed drummers and renamed itself Legion of Mary. They played more than fifty shows in six months before dissolving in July that same year. These were good times for Jerry, John, and the rest of the guys. The more they played, the better they got. The reviews and the turnout kept getting better and better. Making good money changed things on the road; they were able to stay in first-class hotels, eat in the best restaurants, score great drugs, and live the high life. Being on the road with the Jerry Garcia Band, free of an encumbering entourage and complicated politics, differed from touring with the Dead.

In July of 1975, Jerry and John decided to take the band in another direction, looking for a cleaner, leaner sound. John diplomatically parted company with Merl Saunders and saxophonist Martin Fierro, and I persuaded them to drop the incongruous "Legion of Mary" name and just go with the Jerry Garcia Band. Jerry, John, and drummer Ron Tutt needed a keyboard player, someone with exceptional chops, experience, and reputation, as well as the appropriate cool.

## The Chopin of Rock

"Shit, man, do you think he'd want to play with us?" Jerry asked incredulously, after hearing John's suggestion. "I think he'd love to," I replied. "Nicky Hopkins is a great idea."

Nicky was a native of the UK but had recently moved to Mill Valley and was doing session work and performing with Quicksilver Messenger Service. Although he was known primarily for his piano playing with the Stones in the 60s and early 70s, he had become an acclaimed studio musician. In that capacity, he had played on more than three hundred albums and possibly held the distinction of being the greatest rock musician the fewest people had ever heard of.

The guys were anxious to see if he was available, and I jumped right on it. On August 5, 1975, Nicky made his official debut with the Jerry Garcia Band at the Keystone in Berkeley. His virtuoso lyrical style could rock the crowd or seduce them with its elegance, and he was the English romantic prototype—thin, handsome, and profoundly creative. He'd been a musical prodigy and had earned a scholarship to the Royal Academy of Music; his presence in the band inspired everyone. He was a comfortable kind of guy, and in just a few short weeks we felt as if we'd known each other for years. One day I said to Nicky, "Man, your playing is so graceful. I mean, for a guy who's famous as a rock musician, I'm amazed at how you can capture a phrase so eloquently."

Nicky looked at me from beneath the long, flowing amber tresses that framed his delicate features, and said, "I'm going to tell you a secret, Richard."

Really? I was taken aback by this sudden intimacy. "Okay."

"Ever since I was a child learning to play, I have felt this mystical connection to Chopin."

"Really? Chopin? Across time and space. Wow."

"Yeah."

"Amazing, man!" I said, thinking about it a little more. Nicky was quite a character.

Health was one of his biggest challenges. He had Crohn's disease, a miserable congenital intestinal disorder that severely compromised him and was a constant concern. Extended tours had become impossible for him, and he'd told us that the 1972 Stones USA tour had almost done him in. The well-organized and short out-of-town gigs that the Garcia Band was doing seemed to work for him, but before long we started to notice an increase in his reliance on drugs and alcohol. I was amazed that a guy with a major intestinal disorder could pack in so much cocaine and booze, but it seemed to alleviate the symptoms of his affliction; either that or he was just so high he didn't notice them. His self-medicating started to affect his performance and create tensions with the band members, especially Ron, who was Nicky's polar opposite in both physical stature and personality. Nicky was a fragile, capricious Brit and a brilliant musician prone to going off the rails. Ron was a beefy, no-nonsense Texan and a brilliant rock-solid musician. Despite being worlds apart, they had gotten on well at first, but Ron, as the rhythmic center of the band, was intolerant of music inconsistencies. Nicky could be flamboyant, especially when he was loaded, adding an extra beat here and there. These sometimes-sloppy rhythmic fluctuations drove Ron crazy, and I'd see him glaring at the often-oblivious keyboardist.

One night between songs, the band took a quick break, but Nicky remained on stage by himself, conducting a rambling monologue.

"What's he saying?" Jerry asked.

Ron shook his head in disgust. "I don't know, something about fuckin' Chopin! The guy's out of it!"

I knew about Nicky and Chopin, but this was not the time to bring it up. The band had had it with Nicky. His drug and alcohol use debilitated him and made him impossible to work with. His situation was tragic, but the band had no choice but to let him go.

He was a gentle soul who touched me. I was sorry to see him leave the band, and lost contact with him shortly thereafter. In 1994, I heard that he had passed away at the young age of fifty, from complications after intestinal surgery. I was saddened by the news but smiled when I thought that he may have found Chopin in heaven's orchestra.

## The Black, Gay, Junkie Priest

When Nicky left, I had already signed the Jerry Garcia Band to an engagement at Sophie's Club in Palo Alto, so we were pressed to find a replacement. A friend of John's who had been playing in New Orleans suggested that we contact a keyboard guy there named James Booker. He was considered by many esteemed musicians in New Orleans to be the greatest rhythm and blues pianist who ever lived. He was also a mentor to his more well-known contemporaries, Allen Toussaint and Dr. John.

He also had a reputation for being a huge pain in the ass, which made me think I'd have another unstable genius to deal with on the road, but those feelings were put aside and we contacted him. On the phone, despite some misgivings on both our parts, he agreed to a nice chunk of cash, plus expenses, and flew in to play with the guys for the weekend shows at Sophie's.

Booker had a history of drug use dating back to the 60s when he was touring and recording with Lloyd Price, Wilson Pickett, Little Richard, Aretha Franklin, and other artists. After a stint in a band with Dr. John, he had been arrested for possession and served six months in prison. He told me he was on methadone, and I agreed to make arrangements to have it available during his stay in the Bay Area.

On my drive out to the San Francisco airport to pick him up, I figured I wouldn't have a problem recognizing him even though I'd never seen him in person. I knew that he had lost vision in one eye and wore an eye patch, but I wasn't prepared for the guy who walked through the arrival gate. He was a handsome, slender black man wearing a brightly patterned shirt, a red bandana around his head, and a large black leather eye patch with a big white star in the center.

"Hey, James," I said extending my hand, "I'm Richard. Pleased to meet. . ."

"Yeah, yeah," he said, cutting me short. "What about my methadone? An' where am I gonna sleep? Man, I'm hungry! When we gonna eat? Y'all know I'm from N'Orleans and I don't eat no salad shit. Hey, you got my methadone?" I had planned to drive him to John's house in Mill Valley to decompress before the afternoon rehearsal, but I quickly decided that the first stop should be the methadone clinic in San Francisco's Haight-Ashbury neighborhood.

He calmed down after the methadone and accepted my assurances that his needs would be met. I made another stab at some friendly chitchat.

"So, Booker, did you always want to be a musician?"

"Hell no! When I was a boy, I wanted to be a priest."

I almost drove off the road. "A priest?"

"Yeah, can you imagine," he said. "A gay, one-eyed, black ass, junkie priest?"

It was a stretch, I had to admit, but I replied, "Hey, why not? You could play the organ and cruise the confessional." That was the icebreaker. He started opening up in a friendly, funny way that encouraged conversation. He asked me how I got into the business, and I told him about Liberace.

"Ain't that sumthin'! Man, I love Liberace. When I was a kid, I had all his records and learned his solos." He reached inside his coat, took out a card, and handed it to me. The card read: James Booker, the Black Liberace.

The rehearsal and the two club dates that followed went relatively well. The band was amazed by Booker's piano prowess and tolerated his overbearing personality, but it was evident that he was not a good match for the Jerry Garcia Band. He was more of a one-man show than a team player, and he started right in, taking over the session with a flagrant disregard for the other players. Jerry graciously let him run with his own material, and John and Ron made the best of it for those few days, but that was it.

No words can do justice to this man's playing. He was someone you just had to see and hear to truly appreciate. Booker was only a tick of the clock in the history of the Jerry Garcia Band, but he gifted all of us with a display of musicianship that will last forever in our memories. Oh, and I still have the card.

# CHAPTER 19

## RAISING THE DEAD

In June of 1976, the Dead finally decided to end their hiatus and go back on the road. They had not played together as the Grateful Dead for a year and a half.

As their manager, I suggested that they ease back into live performances in smaller venues. With a crew of six instead of twenty, a rented sound system, and significantly reduced transportation costs, the band could net more money. They agreed. I scheduled a couple of shows at the Paramount Theater in Portland, Oregon, and we appointed John Scher as East Coast tour coordinator. He had bailed Jerry out of jail in New Jersey after a pot bust in 1973, which had made him an honorary member of the Dead family. He was trustworthy, intelligent, and efficient, and I liked him and enjoyed working with him. He truly cared about the performers and the fans; he made sure the artists were well treated and the audience got their money's worth.

John booked small-venue shows in Boston, Philadelphia, Chicago, New Jersey, and New York. The weeklong stay in New York included the perk of residing in a posh hotel overlooking Central Park, offered a tasty bite of the Big Apple. I asked Rex Jackson to be road manager. He'd been on the scene a long time, was well respected, and was an asset to the band and, as it turned out, to me as well. In the past, the crew had always been on the attack against management and given me a hard time, but this time, Rex made a point of explaining to the crew the importance of my job, which bolstered my credibility with them.

The tour was a huge success, with sold-out shows everywhere.

We returned to the Northeast in August and did stadium shows in New Jersey and Connecticut, then headed back to Oakland for a two-day, sold-out, outdoor extravaganza with The Who, and finished with a full-blown large-venue tour in October. The fans were thrilled to have the Dead back. The cash flow was great but continued to be a challenge with the expensive tastes and lifestyles that the people on the Grateful Dead Production payroll had become accustomed to.

## Terrapin Station

Things were easing a little financially, but the Grateful Dead Records bankruptcy had to be dealt with and the band no longer had a recording company. We approached Clive Davis, whom I had gotten to know well during my days with the Rowan Brothers, about recording the Dead. Clive, one of the recording industry's best record company presidents, had started his own company, Arista, and was eager to work with the Dead. He felt he could take the band from selling a couple of hundred thousand albums to selling a million. He pitched his deal over lunch at the Beverly Hills Hotel, and we signed a long-term contract. As part of the deal, Clive insisted that an independent producer be brought in to oversee the band's new project, *Terrapin Station*. The band members had no objection when Clive suggested Keith Olsen, who had successfully produced Fleetwood Mac. He was skilled at engineering top-selling albums, and the band spent a good part of early 1977 in a Los Angeles high-tech studio working on the album with Keith.

Jerry took advantage of his time in LA to shuttle between the recording studio and a film-editing lab in Burbank, where he was working on the soundtrack for the *Grateful Dead Movie*. He was enjoying the work, but to get through days and nights of writing, recording, and editing, he had made a pact with the devil.

## Puff of No Return

"Hey, man, you gotta try this shit!" The fateful words rolled off our Persian hash dealer's lips as if he were the snake addressing Eve.

"What is it?" I asked, as Jerry examined the innocuous brown powder that had been placed on my desk in our Mill Valley office.

"It'll mellow you right out," the Persian promised. The scene desperately needed to mellow out. The excessive cocaine use had everyone in a perpetual state of frayed nerves and grinding teeth, and something that would relieve the edginess seemed almost therapeutic. "It's like Persian hash. Take a hit of the smoke," he said, unfolding a small piece of tin foil from his pocket, placing some powder on it, and holding a lighter underneath. We took turns sucking in the smoke with a straw. In a few seconds, we were floating in the warm, comforting balm of heroin. Without a forbidding negative moniker like "smack," it had arrived with an ease of entry, offering a reprieve from all pressures and anxieties— temporarily anyway. Jerry looked at me. "Wow, man, this is some good shit!" I nodded in agreement.

I spent the next couple of days in its comforting clutches but realized the addictive potential of what would later be called "rat." I dipped into it a little every now and then but was fearful of its warm embrace and always partook with great caution. The next time Jerry visited the office, he offered me a puff. I smiled and shook my head,

"I'm holding off on that shit until I'm an old man and my bones start to ache. It's too easy to get strung out on that stuff."

Heroin addiction is insidious, and its destructive power has been described in detail in many places. One of its initial appeals to Jerry was that it helped him balance all his various projects and commitments. He could smoke weed, do coke, take the edge off with rat, record, edit, and perform. He was an easygoing guy who kept an even keel even when he was high. He didn't like theatrics or drama, and rat kept him relaxed and immune to emotional highs and lows. That was true at least for about a year, and then I started to notice some telltale changes. He had a lot less energy, chose to be more reclusive and withdrawn, and had a more passive onstage presence.

Eventually, heroin becomes a consuming drug that users do in seclusion as they slowly slip away. The process can be a long and drawn out or a quick overdose. Jerry did heroin for twenty years, interrupted by futile attempts to clean up. He didn't die of a sudden overdose; heroin just slowly ate away at him like a sweet, suffocating poison.

## The Great Escape

Jerry was not a philanderer, a trait that distinguished him from the typical popular rock star personality. On the road, women and girls always welcomed the opportunity for physical intimacy with a "star." Americans love celebrities, worship fame, and adore idols, but Jerry with his scruffy beard, black jeans, and rumpled black T-shirt didn't cash in that chip. Over the course of his life, he married three times, had four daughters, and loved women in general but was romantically selective.

During the Dead's hiatus, Jerry was struggling to resolve his relationship with Mountain Girl, the mother of two of his children, and an attractive filmmaker, Deborah Koons, whom he had been smitten with since meeting her in New York in 1973. I was sitting in our Mill Valley office one morning when a five-gallon water jug came crashing through the picture window. I dove under my desk. Who'd thrown the fuckin' thing? An insane stalker, a crazed skinhead, a right-wing fanatic?

"Goddamn it, Jerry, I know you're in there. Open this fuckin' door!"

I crawled through the shattered glass and peered over the sill. Outside was an angry Deborah Koons.

"I'm comin' in there, Jerry, you fuckin' asshole," Deborah screamed like a barbarian princess about to breech the walls of Rome.

Suddenly, Jerry ran out of the back bedroom, where he sometimes slept when he was avoiding his romantic dilemmas, clutching his briefcase and intent on escape. He dashed through the door and made an Olympian-quality sprint for his car. Deborah gave chase in a screaming rage, but Jerry humped it across the lawn like a chubby halfback, made it to his car, and roared off. Deborah departed as quickly as she had arrived. Jerry had escaped, Deborah had disappeared, and I was left holding the jug, so to speak, and cleaning up the mess once again.

Jerry later broke off with Deborah and married Mountain Girl in 1981. They divorced twelve years later, and he married Deborah on Valentine's Day 1994, a little more than a year before his death.

# CHAPTER 20

# VISIONS IN GIZA

In 1970, just after I'd arrived in California and was crashing at Marty Balin's place in Mill Valley, I started reading the many books he owned on the lore and legend of Egypt's ancient pyramids on the Giza Plateau. The pyramids and their purpose have inspired esoteric, rich, and imaginative literature with theories ranging from alien outposts to portals of cosmic revelation. Whether they are supernatural vortexes or simply monuments to the immortality of pharaohs, the structures on the Giza Plateau have lured generations of visitors with their wonder and mystery. Experiencing them myself, in all their phenomenal majesty, became one of my life's goals.

Over the years, I continued to read about and plan a visit to Egypt, and when the Dead went on their 1975 hiatus, I decided the time had come to take my trip. In December 1974, a month before my departure, I met Ken Kesey, the founder of the Merry Pranksters and a noted writer. He had just come back from a trip to the pyramids and was chronicling his adventures for Rolling Stone magazine. He gave me some great insights into what I might expect to encounter, and his vivid descriptions sparked my enthusiasm for exotic adventure. The following month, two traveling companions and I flew out of San Francisco, stopped briefly in New York, went on to Rome for a few days, and finally landed in Cairo.

## High Notes

The Cairo airport was an international bazaar—a wild intersection of travelers from all over the world crisscrossing paths without any of the rational, orderly design that organizes and directs wayfarers in big city airports in the Western world. Two of us were dressed in casual California attire and didn't merit a glance from the teeming masses of colorfully dressed Africans, Arabs, and Far Eastern exotics. However, the third member of our party, Goldie—a tall, voluptuous, and regal blonde—attracted numerous sustained appraisals. My European and American travels were sanitized and programmed compared to the organic chaos of this Eastern transport mecca. Franchise coffee shops, generic cafés, leather-upholstered cocktail lounges, and gleaming restrooms were conspicuous in their absence. Finding our luggage was like a treasure hunt. We were directed to an undesignated, crowded space where porters in long, flowing galabias navigated carts loaded with luggage, cardboard boxes, and overflowing shopping bags through a mob of shoving, yelling travelers. From out of the swirling horde, a small Egyptian man, neatly dressed in Western attire, emerged before us. "Excuse me, sir, I drive you and your wives to hotel. I make good price for you."

"Great," I said, "but first we have to find our luggage."

"Richard," Goldie called out, standing out above the crowd on her tiptoes, "it's over there." She pointed to a fast-moving cart on the other side of the room. The little man instructed us to wait and then quickly slipped through the moving maze, targeting our luggage. He was back in short order with our suitcases, and directed us out of the terminal to a parked compact car of unknown origin that he hastily loaded with expert skill. I sat beside our driver, the ubiquitously named Mohammed, while the women sat in the back and stared out the windows at the donkey carts, weaving bicycles, and honking, smoking mass of cars that make up the pandemonium of Cairo traffic. As Mohammed maneuvered through the bumper-to-bumper stream of careening vehicles, he kept glancing in his rearview mirror with undisguised interest. When we stopped momentarily at an intersection, he shifted around and smiled at Goldie. "Hello, Susie," he said.

"Goldie," she replied with a polite nod.

Mohammed resumed driving but gave me an approving glance. "Gold Susie is beautiful woman." I nodded and smiled, captivated by the flow of exotic sights outside my window. He checked the mirror again. "Have breasts round like melon."

"What did he say?" Goldie asked.

"He said you have beautiful eyes," I replied, not wanting our drive to be jeopardized by clashing cultural mores.

"Oh, that's sweet," Goldie said, turning her attention back to Cairo's mix of ancient and modern, East and West.

"Maybe, one day, you let your friend Mohammed take Gold Susie for drive?" His proposition was so outrageous that I had to laugh. "Mohammed very good driver," he assured me. This conversation would be repeated often during our stay in Egypt. A liberated Western woman, traveling alone or with others, was an intriguing and challenging concept for Muslim men. Religion, culture, and lifestyle are intricately connected in the Arab world, and a flamboyant, free spirit like Goldie was a conundrum that could produce both attraction and hostility.

We checked into the Semiramis Hotel, a historic hotel that had not yet undergone modern renovation. Its welcoming shabbiness and old-world charm offered a relaxed elegance missing in newly constructed hotels. Situated in the European Quarter on the city's right bank, the locale had been transformed into an upscale enclave of hotels, banks, universities, museums, and consulates. In the streets and the architecture, you could see the footprints of Assyrian, Persian, Greek, Roman, Ottoman, French, and British invaders, whose influences had been assimilated into the city's fascinating cultural layering. Cairo's vitality was best experienced in places such as the Khan el-Khalili market, where commerce is carried on with exuberance and the clamoring and commotion of bargaining is equal parts business and theater. Like a Technicolor movie, Cairo flashed scenes of turbaned men sharing hookahs, playing cards, and drinking tea in side street cafés beside slaughtered sheep, hooked and hanging in butcher shop doorways. Women, silent and veiled, wove mysteriously past gesticulating merchants with a cacophony of urban noise in the background. Vehicle exhaust, roasted meats, sweet perfumes, unwashed bodies, and the pervasive wafting smoke of aromatic tobacco comingled into one mind-blowing, crazed sensory experience. We inhaled it as if it were the spent passion of an exotic and world-weary lover.

## Shemi's Girl

I have smoked cannabis in various forms in my adult years and am a confirmed pothead who enjoys its varied pleasures from pleasant to transfixing. Just as a whiskey connoisseur visiting Ireland wants to sample the best in local spirits, I wanted a puff of Egypt's finest. Hashish had been artfully cultivated in the East for centuries, but a westerner procuring it had to use extreme caution and discretion. Those were not two of my greatest virtues, but I was determined to have a go anyway.

One afternoon a couple of days after we arrived, I sauntered down to the hotel bar. The lounge resembled Rick's Café Américain in *Casablanca*, complete with a venerable-looking bartender in a bow tie and short-waisted maroon jacket. It was early and the room was deserted, so I pulled up a stool and ordered a Guinness. The bartender, Shemi, was an old-world hospitality professional whose manner was as smooth and comforting as a shot of the good stuff after a long, hard day. Over salted nuts and a beer, we chatted about everything from pyramids to politics. After my second Guinness, I leaned over the bar and said, "You know, Shemi, back in the States we are discovering something that your people have known for centuries."

He smiled knowingly and nodded, "Yes, it's true, we found out long ago that too many wives are a problem."

"Well, that too," I said with a laugh, "but I was actually thinking about hashish."

"Oh, hashish is a woman, too, but not a wife. She is, how you say? A girlfriend, yes?"

"Exactly. Do you think you could possibly introduce me to such a girl?"

"Most Egyptian men have such a girlfriend," he said, reaching into his pocket and pulling out a small piece of hashish that he guardedly placed beneath a napkin and slid over to me.

"Aha," I said. "Egypt's finest!

"No, no—we get from Lebanon."

"What about Egyptian hash?" I asked.

"No hash Egypt," he said, shaking his head.

Back in my room, I embraced Shemi's girlfriend with her soft, sweet tan color and intoxicating scent. She satisfied all my fantasies.

## High Notes

With his kind help, my affair transformed many otherwise ordinary evenings into languid, smoky, romantic interludes. I will never forget Shemi or his beautiful, blonde Lebanese girlfriends.

After a few days in Cairo, we felt culturally acclimatized enough to leave the city and take a trip to the pyramids of Giza, about twenty miles to the south. After a dusty taxi ride, we checked into the Mena House, a legendary hotel that has hosted world travelers, presidents, and pop stars. The views of the pyramids from the hotel and its grounds are stunning, and you can walk to the base of the pyramids in minutes.

Visitors at the pyramids are besieged by swarms of guides and drivers offering their services. Kesey had warned me that they were all professional hustlers but had added that striking the right rapport with one would be immensely helpful in navigating the sights, negotiating with merchants, being shielded from incessant peddlers and beggars, and arranging adventures off the beaten path. We walked over to the pyramids and maneuvered through the throng of guides, vendors, and con men. About fifty feet from our destination, I heard a voice say, "Excuse me, mister. Can you help me, please?" Polite, neatly dressed, and speaking adequate English, he introduced himself. His name was Nasr and his ploy was not to come on as a guide but to ask our help in translating a letter from a friend in London. He couldn't have been more transparent, but I liked his style and resourcefulness and negotiated with him to be our local guide, personal assistant, and tour director. He quickly demonstrated his worth by bribing the gatekeeper at the entrance to the pyramids so we could have a private tour. To attune my senses to all the arcane nuances of ancient knowledge and mystery, I called on my Lebanese girlfriend and had a smoke. After the tour, Nasr arranged a visit on horseback to several of the region's country villages, where life seemed to be passing at a timeless pace. We stopped in one of them for lunch, and were approached by an elderly man who was selling postcards; he spoke a little English, and I asked him to join us.

"Thank you, my friend. Where are you from?"

"California," I replied, rather than "America," because I had noticed that people associated California with glamour and the good life and America with the hard edge of money and power.

He nodded. "Are you playboy?"

I laughed. "No, are you?"

Returning my smile, he said, "No, I'm old man, eighty-eight years old. I am sometimes farmer, sometimes fisherman, take care of the animals, watch my family."

"How many children?"

"Ten."

"So many!" I exclaimed. "You sell postcards to help take care of them?"

"No, they take care of me. I sell postcards so I can talk to visitors, people from everywhere. It is my great joy, in my old age, the world comes to me."

These fleeting but memorable encounters with ordinary Egyptians were recurring pleasures. In some of these unexpected moments, a remarkable, genuine exchange took place that left me with a deep conviction about our shared humanity. On a crowded New York subway, people try hard to ignore each other, but people here were open and receptive.

These spontaneous interactions were often the highlight of my day and sustained my enthusiasm for the journey.

## Prophesy by Moonlight

One evening, Nasr arranged for us to take a horseback ride around the Sphinx. The pyramids of Giza were in the background, and it was a beautiful night with a necklace of stars that lined up perfectly beneath a bright pendant moon. A few quick visits to my Lebanese girlfriend heightened my appreciation of the energy valances emanating from the site. I was dreamily falling under the spell of Giza's mystery when I noticed a large wooden stage on the desert sands at the foot of the monuments. I didn't know why it was there, probably for official government ceremonies, but the sight of a stage in this legendary location triggered my imagination. On that very stage beneath those carefully aligned stars, I envisioned the Grateful Dead playing and singing their melodic odes to the ages. The music swirled around the Sphinx and the pyramids, a sinuous fabric of sound connecting the ancient and modern worlds. Even though I knew it wasn't real, I imagined the scene with an extraordinary clarity. The vision stayed etched in my mind; even now, when I close my eyes and conjure up the image, it returns more as a spiritual guide than as a physical memory.

Most of us have experienced a moment of unexplainable mystery—perpetuated perhaps by trauma, drugs, or extreme circumstances—carrying an indubitable truth and power. Whether from hashish or the numinous energy of that ancient place, that night in February 1975 would lead to the defining moment of my career in the music industry. I knew I would one day be quitting the business, but I knew also that I had to make that visionary moment a living reality.

## Spirit of the Nile

We left Mena the next day and flew to Luxor on the Nile, the site of the magnificent ruins at Karnak. When we arrived, I discovered that I had lost my Lebanese girlfriend! I was disappointed and longed for the subtle enhancement that she provided.

From our hotel in the late afternoon, I could see a fleet of small open boats called feluccas floating on the nearby Nile, their white triangular sails ruffling in the breeze. I strolled down to the riverbank, where a group of desert sailors greeted me. After a few minutes of casual conversation, I inquired about purchasing a small amount of hash. They smiled and nodded and talked of the head boatman, Abdul Atti, pointing out the location of his boat, the *Gazelle*, in the distance on the river. They told me that they would arrange a meeting and to come back in the early evening. When I returned at dusk, crimson clouds reflected in the water, transforming the river into a ribbon of scarlet. The last rays of the sun danced off the polished wood of the *Gazelle*, and from its deck, a man in an immaculate white galabia motioned me aboard.

My host was a small man with chiseled features and a luxurious black mustache. With an air of quiet dignity, he lowered his head as I approached and said, "As-salamu alaykum."

"As-salamu alaykum," I replied, completing the traditional "peace be upon you" greeting. I was unsure of how to proceed, but he put me at ease with his smile and ushered me to an embroidered cushion, where I sat as the *Gazelle* slipped silently into the languid current and glided onto the sunset river. Without discussion, he handed me hashish, a small wooden pipe smooth from the touch of many hands, and a glass cup filled with hot tea and several cubes of sugar. We smoked, drank tea, and floated slowly down river. My anxiety and constant sense of urgency, a residue of the entertainment business, slipped overboard and sank beneath the serenity of the Nile.

"How long have you been a boatman, Atti?"

"All my life, just as my father before me."

I told him how generations of my family had worked the vineyards of Italy, distilling and selling wine.

"Is wine still your family's trade?"

"Yes," I replied. "In America now though. America is a place people go to start a new life."

Atti nodded. "Here we follow the old ways. They run deep and keep their own time like the rhythms of the river." Indeed, time had slowed its relentless pace as we shared our histories and spoke freely from our hearts long after the sun had set. When the *Gazelle* returned to shore, I had the extraordinary feeling that I had lost the hash to find something much greater.

Before parting company, I arranged a four-day voyage on the *Gazelle* to Aswan. During that trip, my bond with Atti grew stronger and I confided my dream of staging a Grateful Dead concert at the pyramids of Giza. He encouraged me to make my vision a reality and offered to introduce me to his influential friends in the Egyptian tourism industry. He joined us on our flight back to Cairo and made good on his offer. Within days of our return, I was pitching my concept to the director of the Ministry of Tourism. Everything was lining up just like the stars on that moonlit night. I knew I would have to work hard to make the concerts happen, but I no longer considered my vision a dream. I trusted that I had been given this opportunity and was determined to see it realized.

## Men in Dark Suits

"What? Promote the Grateful Dead in Egypt? You gotta be crazy!" Bill Graham shouted when I approached him with my idea. It was fall 1977, two years after my first visit to Egypt, and I felt that the time was now or never.

"I'm a Holocaust survivor, for Chrissakes," Graham moaned. "You want me to help you take the band to a place where they hate my people? Besides, there's a fucking war going on over there!"

"There's no war going on," I assured him. "The timing is perfect. I've been monitoring the scene. Sadat has thrown out the Russian military and is getting U.S. aid. The Egyptian people love America." It was going to be a hard sell, but I persisted. "Listen, if we pull this off, it would be a major coup for you—a cross-cultural music event that would eclipse anything that's ever been done. There's even a stage there already." I saw the promise of showbiz glory catching his attention.

He nodded. "We could maybe do a double bill with Santana."

There was no way I was going to let another group share the stage with the Dead, and I knew the band would never go for it. "This has got to be a Grateful Dead solo venture. You yourself said—'the Grateful Dead are not the best at what they do; they're the only ones who do what they do!'" Despite my best arguments, and those of several members in the band, Bill remained skeptical. Suddenly I had a revelation: Why give to Bill Graham what could be the biggest international event in rock history? The thought of him grandstanding and taking control over my vision was all I needed to motivate me to try another approach.

I enlisted Alan Trist, a good friend and trusted management associate, and we began to make inquiries at a Washington-based consultant company. They helped us set up a cocktail party at a ritzy Washington hotel for young diplomats from the United States and Egypt to further our project. Our committee—Alan, Phil Lesh, and I—had to lose our laid-back California look and don appropriate attire to schmooze the foreign-relations diplomats, and we became known as the MIDS, the Men in Dark Suits. Whether it was the suits, the booze, or simply the merits of the project, the party was a success.

We were starting to attract the right attention, and we MIDS continued to build momentum with an encouraging visit to the Egyptian ambassador's office. The adventure found us flying to Cairo, where our dark suits and ties were a challenge in the hot sticky weather. We persevered, giving donations to appropriate charities and participating in a series of protocol meetings with various Egyptian and American officials and diplomats. Our efforts paid off by getting us a decisive meeting with Saad el Din, the Egyptian minister of culture. "Do you think music changes in different places?" Saad el Din, who was himself a musician and a poet, asked Phil.

Phil didn't miss a beat. "Certainly. That's why we are excited and honored at the prospect of playing at your auspicious site."

Bingo. Shortly afterward, we were able to telegraph the Grateful Dead office that the deal had been sealed! The Grateful Dead would play three concerts at the pyramids of Giza in September 1978.

# CHAPTER 21

# DESERT DREAMS

We MIDS returned from Egypt in March 1978.

Word of the concerts had spread quickly through the Dead community. The atmosphere was charged with excitement, and we were nervous about word getting out to the general public too early. We had learned that several similar events, whose early promotions brought attention, had been cancelled in diplomatically sensitive countries because of security concerns. Bill Graham, for one, had tried to promote a big-time rock concert in the Soviet Union that was cancelled mysteriously. He, of all people, should have known the importance of keeping a low profile about plans. With his close connections to the Dead family, he was one of the first to hear that we had been able to cut through all the red tape bullshit. He was all over it: Not only did he change his mind about not wanting to be any part of it, but he tried to step in as a major player, offering his connections and influence. His enthusiasm was drawing the exact attention we were trying to avoid, and we had to ask Uncle Bill to back off. We decided not to make an official announcement about the concerts until right before leaving at the end of the summer.

## Ladies, Gentlemen, and Deadheads: A Special Announcement

The September 2, 1978 concert at Giant Stadium in East Rutherford,

New Jersey, was the last show before Egypt. We MIDS distributed a press release there and set up a post-concert news conference to elaborate on the upcoming Giza extravaganza. It was an unfamiliar format for all of us, but we answered questions from the media as best we could.

"Why do you want to play at the pyramids?"

Phil took the question. "The way we play is affected by where we play. The pyramid site is one of the world's greatest power centers."

After a series of predictable questions and sincere replies, a reporter asked, "What was the biggest obstacle you had to overcome?"

"The biggest challenge for me," I replied, "was to negotiate an earth-moon alignment that would result in a lunar eclipse during the final performance on Saturday, the 16th of September." That lightened the mood, and I added, "In all seriousness, we originally contracted for two shows and then added a third, not knowing that an eclipse was going to occur that night. In an independent venture of this magnitude, financing is always the biggest obstacle. We're throwing our fate to the wind." These words proved all too prophetic.

## Karma in the Details

The reign of the neo-cocaine cowboys was over, but the crew still maintained the tradition of excluding newcomers from what they deemed was their realm of exclusive acceptance and privilege.

Keith Godchaux, the band keyboardist, needed his piano tuned before each performance. This service was masterfully done by a tuner recruited by John Scher. The tuner was not a regular member of the Dead crew and he was mercilessly hazed by the backstage boys who made a habit of greedily indulging their sense of self-empowerment with aggressive bullying. This abuse reached a boiling point at the Giant Stadium concert, when the tuner's parents were denied privileged access to the stage to watch the show with their son. It was the last affront the tuner would tolerate, and he quit.

I was not aware of the incident until we were on-site in Egypt and I asked where the guy was. It was impossible to find a local replacement in Egypt, and the quality of the band's music was seriously compromised by an out-of-tune piano. The upshot was, when the band returned home and listened to the performance recordings, they were not pleased with the sound and vetoed releasing a live album. The decision dealt a fatal blow to the finances. The original plan had been to recoup the cost of the trip with the album; not doing that left us half a million dollars in the hole. The ego-driven, petty snobbery of the self-imagined backstage gatekeepers had a huge price.

## Sand Trap

The Egypt concerts were a challenge in more ways than one. The first major challenge was how to get a sound system worthy of the event to the site.

Transporting a huge system from the United States was too costly. I remembered that when The Who weren't on tour, they rented out their sound system and recording equipment. I contacted their manager and made the necessary arrangements. The equipment had to be shipped by freighter from England to Alexandria, Egypt's northernmost port. Those arrangements were easy compared to getting the equipment from there to the site because there were no established trucking companies that could do the job. We had to use our Cairo connections to locate a couple of big rigs for the overland transport. The trucks picked up our cargo without any problems and miraculously made it over one hundred fifty potholed miles from Alexandria to Mena. With their destination near, they cut across the desert sands, lost traction, and sank down, unable to go any farther. There were no vehicles around that could possibly pull them out, so we ended up having the local herders pull the trucks out with their camels. The equipment finally arrived at the site to the thunderous applause of the waiting crew of Americans and Egyptians, and everyone sprang into action to set things up. Without benefit of a common language, they figured out the installation with universal gestures and hand signals worthy of a United Nations promotional video on international cooperation. In total, transporting and installing the sound system took more than a month; it was only one of the many unpredictable contingencies typical of every aspect of the project.

The Dead family, who had known about the concerts long before the official announcement, had every intention of making the trip. It was a big happening in the Dead scene and almost everybody wanted to go. We were besieged with requests for travel and hotel information.

Randy Sarti, the Dead's steadfast travel agent, was fortunately skilled and experienced when it came to dealing with the extraordinary demands of rock 'n' roll bands. He came up with the idea of chartering flights and block-booking hotel rooms at the Mena House, across from the pyramids, to accommodate fifty or so friends and family members. It was no small feat given the finite number of available rooms and interminable requests. The Mena House had seen wars, plagues, and sandstorms, but accommodating the invading Deadheads might have been its most challenging and otherworldly experience.

"Hello, room service?"

"This is the front desk. We don't have room service at three o'clock in the morning."

"Well hey man, can ya send out for a dozen cheeseburgers? We've got a serious case of the munchies!"

"What are munchies, please? Do you need a doctor?"

"No, we need cheeseburgers!"

"What is cheeseburger, please?"

## Documenting the Adventure

Long before the official announcement, word of the trip also had reached a filmmaker who wanted to shoot the event as a concert epic. He contacted me with a proposal and an offer. The band discussed the pros and cons, but Jerry was against it. In his mind, the trip was a vacation for family and friends, and he thought the presence of an outside film crew would be disruptive and change the relaxed atmosphere. He was adamant about his decision, but it started me thinking that maybe it was important to chronicle the once-in-a-lifetime performance.

I was thinking about using a handheld Super 8 camera, which would produce a home-movie kind of result. Jerry liked the idea and was open to my bringing along a Japanese friend who knew a lot more about filming than I did. His contributions to the filming were invaluable.

We shot a lot of film and captured many wonderful moments throughout the days we were there. The concerts drew local attention, and a Cairo television station sent cameramen to shoot footage at all the shows. On the last night, it dawned on me that some of that professional footage would be great for our archives. I happened to have a thousand bucks in my pocket, and I approached one of the TV cameramen, who traded his film for my money. With that footage and my footage, I had a significant amount of material for a documentary. However, the project was shelved and unshelved over the years, and finally came out only in an abbreviated form years later as *The Vacation Tapes*, a bonus segment on the Rhino Records DVD titled *Rocking the Cradle*.

I hope that someday the unseen footage will be available for everyone to see.

## Deadheads, Pranksters, and a Redheaded Giant

Many travelers arrived at the Mena House days before the concerts and had a chance to relax, unwind, and acclimate. Every day, a new collection of varied and colorful characters arrived: Dedicated Deadheads from around the world networked their way there one way or another. Kesey showed up with members of the Merry Pranksters and a small video camera crew to document their experiences. Bill Walton, the NBA basketball star and a huge Deadhead, stole the scene with his towering height, mop of curly red hair, and cast on his broken foot. Everyone felt at home and relaxed in the shadows of the pyramids.

The Pranksters climbed to the top of the Great Pyramid, planted a Grateful Dead flag, and captured it forever on film. Climbing the pyramids is illegal, but with a small bribe, the Egyptians overseeing the site happily look the other way. Deadheads and locals got high together, and a spirit of conviviality and friendship kept the atmosphere relaxed and playful.

One afternoon poolside, the well-known alternative journalist Paul Krassner found drummer Bill Kreutzmann in good humor, sitting with the Great Pyramid behind him as a backdrop, and began a mock interview. I grabbed my cassette recorder and joined the faux news conference, to record it for posterity:

Krassner: Of all the impressions you've had of being here, what's the most outstanding?

Kreutzmann: Well, there is this big block of blocks (he said pointing to the Great Pyramid) and they're a little loose. I've done a lot of checking and measuring and I find a few flaws in the overall structure of the pyramid, ones that don't meet the eye. The only way you know about them is by sound. I found that when the bass plays a certain note along with the high cymbal, there's a slight combeline [a made-up nonsense word] in the center. So I believe the pyramid was built for the reason of hiding or disguising a vehicle.

Krassner: Like the Green Hornet vehicle?

Kreutzmann: No. More like a modern-day flying saucer that was made thousands of years ago . . . You know the pyramid is not a tomb, man, you know that; it's actually a disguise for a fantastic, beautiful, gleaming, glistening, glowing flying saucer. I believe it's located about two-thirds up above the King's Chamber, but no one's gone there because they don't want to dig through. One of these nights, probably on the night of the full moon in eclipse, the band and the audience will touch chords and the pyramid will slowly unfasten itself, and piece by piece and block by block, it will slowly crumble away, revealing the most gleaming and beautiful flying saucer—and that's the great plan and that's why we're over here.

## Tears of Joy

Opening night, the lights came up on stage, illuminating the Grateful Dead members and the words *EGYPT 1978* emblazoned across the front edge of the stage. The pyramids and the Sphinx were aglow in the background. Tears streamed down my face as I sobbed uncontrollably. Some reservoir deep within me overflowed with an uncontainable joy. My dream had become a reality in the purest sense, and I felt an overwhelming emotion that I had never felt before—or since.

Hamza El Din, the Nubian vocalist and internationally famous musician, opened the show playing his oud, a twelve-string predecessor of the lute. Ten Nubian hand-clappers accompanied by ten tar drummers from Hamza's village joined him on stage and the mood was mystical.

Before too long, Jerry came in on the melody above the drumming and clapping and was joined by Weir and the remaining band members as they segued into "Not Fade Away." I glanced at the audience in the front row, where the seats had been reserved for Egyptian dignitaries, who were formally dressed in suits and looked a little bewildered by the amplified music and the entire phenomenon but were trying to figure it all out. One or two songs into the set, the dancing Deadheads took over the area in front of the stage, with Egyptian students, Mena village locals, and the desert Bedouins checking it all out from the sidelines. It was the first of three triumphant shows.

As the show came to a close on the final night, I stood on the stage basking in the euphoria of the moment. Most everyone by then had taken a hit or more of acid from the Pranksters' Murine bottle, and magic was in the air. The full moon in lunar eclipse had just captivated us with its cosmic magnificence, and the vibe on the stage was electric. The pyramids rising from the desert sands behind us and the Sphinx all aglow and seated majestically to our left were fucking awesome to behold! While we were still on stage, the news reached us that Egyptian President Anwar El Sadat, Israeli Prime Minister Menachem Begin, and U.S. President Jimmy Carter had just announced the Camp David Peace Accords, which was the closest they'd ever come to achieving peace in the Middle East. The universe was smiling on that historic night!

## Uncle Bill's Big Party

I was shaken from my delirious reverie by the sight of some fifty saddled camels and tethered horses on the fringe of the desert. Good old Uncle Bill! He had flown in a couple of days before the show to witness the desert happenings—he had to be part of it all!

Taken by the magnitude and significance of the event, he wanted in on the glory and was staging a Bill Graham Presents show all its own. He had arranged to have the camels, horses, and guides converge at the show's end and escort everyone across the sands to a village in the Sahara Desert a few miles west of the concert site. He had erected a huge tent there and put on a desert bacchanal, replete with belly dancers, the finest local food, and imported alcoholic beverages. The affair lasted until the desert sun peeked over the dunes, an appropriately enchanting ending to our Egypt concert series.

## A Moment in Time

After the shows, Jerry, Bobby, Keith, Donna, Alan, about twenty close family members of the band, and I sailed for two and a half days up the Nile from Luxor to Aswan on Atti's new boat, the

*Sobek*—dubbed the "Ship of Fools." Other members of the group flew to Luxor and visited the Valley of the Kings. Mickey Hart and a recording and engineering team headed off deep into Upper Egypt to Hamza El Din's hometown, where they shared musical heritages and recorded the results. Without question, this was a sweet spot in time and a unique chapter in the Grateful Dead chronicles.

When we returned home, we received a note from Ashraf Ghorbal, the Egyptian ambassador to the United States:

"The accounts in both the Egyptian and the American press, plus the reports I have received regarding the success of your September concerts at the Sphinx Theater, give me, as they must give you and your colleagues, great satisfaction. It is an historic "first" in the annals of modern music—to play the Pyramids before thousands of fans, old and new. These concerts have become a unique chapter in the story of Egyptian-American friendship and we are pleased and gratified that the proceeds of the ticket sales went to the Faith and Hope Society and the Department of Antiquities. They will be put to very good use. My sincere congratulations and best wishes of success to the Grateful Dead."

Wow!

# CHAPTER 22

# KEEPING THE PEDAL TO THE METAL

After we returned from Egypt, events moved at a hectic pace. Jerry and the band nixed releasing any music from the pyramid concerts, eliminating that moneymaking possibility, so there was a crucial need for a busy performance schedule to support the band's free-spending lifestyle.

In October, I booked five shows in San Francisco at Winterland and billed them the "From Egypt with Love" concerts. It was one way to reap some financial rewards from our Egypt expedition, and the band was eager to share their experiences with the fans. I wanted to present some of the more than thirty hours of footage from the trip but didn't have enough time to wrestle it into a coherent film. Instead, I collected several hundred slides from people who had taken shots on the trip and had them projected one by one on a huge screen behind the band as they performed. The slide show was a big success and the audience broke out in applause over and over again.

In November, we headed to New York, kicking off an East Coast tour with an appearance on *Saturday Night Live*. The band had recently completed their *Shakedown Street* album and performed "Casey Jones" and a medley from the album. The *Saturday Night Live* cast and the band hit it off, and they returned to do a second show in Spring 1980, feeling a lot less pressured, relaxed, and comfortable. Seeing Belushi, Ackroyd, and Murray again was like reuniting with old friends, and we all ended up at Ackroyd and Belushi's private club, partying until the wee hours. They were party animals, and the Dead had met their match.

## One Sweet Woman

"I read somewhere, I think it was Edgar Cayce, that the ancient people of Atlantis who escaped the destruction of their civilization made it to Egypt and were responsible for building the Great Pyramid."

Wow! I had stumbled out of the maelstrom of the *Saturday Night Live* cocktail party and grabbed a chair at a small table on the fringe of the madness without noticing the delicate, attractive woman on the other side. I did a double take and recognized her, all the more amazed by her statement on Egyptology.

"What do you think of that theory?" she asked.

I was taken by her and pulled myself together enough to answer. "Well, after my several visits, I find it impossible to believe that the Great Pyramid was built by ordinary slave labor. There are lots of theories about its purpose and who built it. I don't buy the theory that it was Cheops's tomb."

We introduced ourselves and kept on chatting while the party raged on beyond. I was fascinated by her gentle smile and unassuming demeanor. We seemed to connect effortlessly.

"I think as a species we've lost more than the secrets of ancient technology; we've lost our spiritual bearings."

I nodded in agreement, trying not to make my total infatuation too obvious.

She continued. "We're warring, ego-driven people. While we profess to be against war, we can't see the connection between what takes place on the battlefield and how violent and competitive we are with each other in our everyday lives. It's the same emotion. The difference lies only in degrees."

I felt as if I'd met my soul mate! She was making quite an impression on me. I was enjoying our conversation so much I was about to suggest getting together again sometime when a stumbling party fugitive planted his fist on the table, almost overturning it. It was John Belushi. His face was bright with a smile, and he was waving a glass around. "C'mon, Gilda," he teased in his irrepressible way, "you used to be a lotta fun! Join the party!"

Gilda Radner stood and gave him an affectionate peck, "Thanks, John," she said, smiling, "but I really need to be going." Then she turned to me and took my hand. "So nice meeting you. I hope I haven't bored you with all my talk." Before I could beg her to stay, Belushi croaked, "Hey, one dance! I know you love to swing it! C'mon!"

"I'm just not a big party person," she said.

"Ah! Okay! If ya gotta go," Belushi said with resignation. John put me in a bear hug and tugged me toward the rollicking crowd and party festivities.

"You need a drink, buddy!" Belushi said, laughing and dragging me toward the bar.

I slid out from under his grip and looked back. Just before disappearing into the crowd, Gilda turned slightly and smiled at me over her shoulder. Now she was gone. Oh man, I wanted to run after her and. . . and . . . as Emily Litella would say, "Never mind!"

## One Strong Woman

In December 1978, my secretary picked up a call and announced, "Richard, Jane Fonda for you!"

"You know," I said, going along with what I thought must be a gag, "I only take calls from Faye Dunaway."

"Seriously! Really?"

"Yes!"

I picked up the phone and in a disbelieving tone said, "Hello?"

"Hi, Richard, this is Jane Fonda. I got your name from Bill Graham, and I'm hoping you can help me out. I'm trying to raise money for my husband Tom Hayden's Campaign for Economic Democracy, and I'm hoping you can convince the Grateful Dead to do a benefit concert."

She wasn't wasting any time getting to the point. "Can you tell me a little about the organization?" I queried.

"The Campaign for Economic Democracy has twenty-five state-wide chapters. It works with neighborhood organizations, the trade union movement, and activists in California's minority communities in an attempt to build a progressive coalition to fight big business and bureaucratic government. At the moment, they're focusing on promoting solar energy, environmental protection, and renter's rights. Our governor, Jerry Brown, is working closely with Tom on these issues."

Yowza! She sounded like a recording.

"I can't promise anything," I said. "It seems like a worthy cause, but I have to tell you upfront that the band, as a rule, is apolitical. You probably recall how they distanced themselves from the Students for a Democratic Society and the Berkeley radical activists in the 60s. I think it's tough sell, but I'd be happy to run the idea by them."

Without a pause, she added, "Perhaps it would help if I could speak with them personally and explain what it is we're trying to achieve."

I couldn't imagine that happening.

"Let me try first. They're on a tour in the South right now, but I'll talk to them about it as soon as they get back. They'll be playing in LA for a night just before the New Year. Maybe I can arrange for you to meet with them then."

"Perfect. I'm shooting a movie now with Lily Tomlin and Dolly Parton. Why don't you come down a day or so early, and we can meet at the studio and talk more about it."

I took her number and promised to call.

The movie was *Nine to Five*, and I flew down to Los Angeles the day before the concert to meet Jane on the set and watch the shoot.

The film was a comedy about three secretaries who were revolting against their sexist boss, and Jane's co-stars, Dolly and Lily, were there as well. The afternoon on the set with the three ladies was special and enjoyable but too hectic to discuss the benefit with Jane. I suggested that she come by the Dead's sound check the next day.

When the band gathered at the venue, I told them Jane was stopping by, which caused some eye rolling. However, Mickey and Bobby were more interested and sought me out after the announcement.

"Hey, Richard, make sure you let me know as soon as she arrives," Mickey requested.

"Will do, but I gotta warn you, she's gonna try and recruit you."

"We can handle her," Mickey boasted. "We're used to people coming onto us."

"Did she tell you what she wants?" Bobby was in on the conversation too.

"Yeah, kind of. Hayden's using her celebrity to raise bucks for worthy causes. You know, like fighting big business, supporting unions, promoting solar energy . . . shit like that."

"Well, she better have a strong pitch. We don't support politicians, and we're not an easy sell," Mickey replied.

"We don't impress easy. We've been around," Bobby tacked on, quickly adding, "When's she getting here?"

"I don't know. Soon."

"Well, bring her to us when she comes," he said, walking away.

Sure, they'd been around, but Jane had been around too. She wasn't there long before they fell under her spell like everyone else, including Bill Graham, had. The woman had brains, beauty, and charisma—and she knew how to use it all. She got her way, of course, and the band did a concert we called "The Rock for Life" in support of environmentalists against the polluting corporations. The fans, however, weren't used to waiting for the music to begin, and even Jane and her husband Tom Hayden's intensity couldn't tame the fired-up Deadhead audience. They had no patience with the passionate, pre-concert spiel, and we got the two activists off the stage just before things threatened to turn ugly.

The Campaign for an Economic Democracy ended up getting fifteen thousand dollars, Bobby and Mickey got to schmooze with Jane, and as much as I liked her, I told my secretary, "If Jane calls again, I'm out of the office."

## The Yin and Yang of Bill Graham

Bill Graham was a complex guy, and my relationship with him was equally complex. Much of Bill's tenacity and aggressiveness stemmed from an incredibly difficult childhood. He had lost his mother in the Holocaust and barely escaped to the United States. He was a survivor who grew up tough and smart on the streets of New York and eventually found his way to San Francisco, where he made a name for himself both as a music promoter and as a force to be reckoned with.

When I was the agent for Jefferson Airplane, during my early days in New York at APA, Bill was the Airplane's manager. He gave me possible booking time slots and then rejected or accepted my proposed offers based on the venue and the promoter's guarantee to the artist. Booking the Airplane was the big break that helped me segue into representing other big-time rock bands, and I appreciated his help. By the time I was appointed the Grateful Dead's agent and general manager eight years later, Bill had become the golden boy of entrepreneurial rock 'n' roll emulated by promoters nationwide. He had also earned a reputation for unscrupulously exploiting bands financially.

As manager of one of those bands, I had to keep a close eye on him, as much as I hated to do so. True to what I'd heard, I found he was padding expenses, undercounting the gate, and trying to pull off a bunch of other unethical practices. Bill knew how to charm the artists and was their backstage buddy. He impressed them with his creative pairing of musical acts and the promotion of worthy benefit concerts. My relationship with him was different. I was hired by the Dead to manage their financial affairs and couldn't ignore what he was doing. The band knew about his practices through me, but we could do little short of refusing to work with him. Bill and I fought tooth and nail for years until I was finally worn down and at my wit's end. In April 1979, just before a show in San Jose, his cheating finally sent me over the edge, and I was hellbent to get out from under any dealings with him. I called John Scher. "I'm fuckin' fed up! I can't deal with Graham any longer. He's jerking me around with the expenses, trying to pull things over on me right and left, and driving me fuckin' nuts! I'll give you my agent's fee if you strike the deal! I've had it with the fucking crook!"

"God! I'd like to help you out, but there's no way I can get involved without Bill's consent," John responded.

"Do whatever you have to do. I've had it!"

At first Bill was thrilled to have me out of the picture; he welcomed John's involvement, but he underestimated him. The tickets had gone on sale but Bill still hadn't submitted the expenses. John called him to ask why he hadn't received them. Bill unloaded on him in no uncertain terms.

In Dennis McNally's book, *Long Strange Trip,* the Dead biographer quotes Scher recounting his experience: "It was my first experience with a Bill roar. He went berserk, 'I have to deal with a fuckin' Jersey asshole to book my band? You motherfuckin' ingrate scumbag.' It was a nonstop lunatic binge for twenty minutes, and then a hang-up. I called Loren, and said I quit. The Dead did the gig, but from then on my relationship with Bill was acrimonious."

Speaking truth to power hurt me in the long run. Two years down the line, after I had resigned from the Dead, I offered Bill a major share in a moneymaking movie-music venture that he refused not from a business point of view but from lingering resentment. It was an unfortunate situation.

Bill died in a helicopter crash in 1991 at the young age of sixty. He was a larger-than-life personality who defied categorization, contrasting his shady business practices with great personal generosity, his combativeness with compassion, and his vulgarity with sensitivity. I will always have mixed feelings about Bill and will never forget him. God bless.

> *Do I contradict myself?*
> *Very well then I contradict myself,*
> *I am large,*
> *I contain multitudes.*
> Walt Whitman, *Song of Myself*

## The Flying Mule

We were flying hundreds of feet above the rugged Alaskan landscape when Sumner Putman, our dashing young bush pilot, looked over at me with a mischievous twinkle in his eyes and said, "Wanna do a loop-de-loop? It's a kick! Just don't tell anybody. It's dangerous. Hell of a lot of fun though!"

In April 1980, Deborah, my longtime partner; Gus, my seven-year-old son from a previous marriage; and I were soaring above the snowy Alaskan plains—guests of the Alaskan promoter George Lichter. George wanted the Grateful Dead to put on a series of summer solstice shows in Anchorage, and I thought they might be a perfect follow-up to Egypt. The limited facilities at the available venue were not up to the band's technical standards, however, and they had vetoed the deal, but George was not easily discouraged and arranged for me to visit the Great North. He was hoping that I would be enthused after experiencing the wonders of Alaska, and would convince the band to change their mind. High above the wilderness in a single-engine Cessna with Sumner and me in the front seats and Deborah and Gus on inverted oil drums in the back, we were getting a taste of Alaska's vastness and beauty. I'm not one for daredevil risks and would probably have declined Sumner's offer, but Gus was pleading, "C'mon, Dad, remember the glider?" Gus, Deborah, and I had been on a glider flight the previous month and done a thrilling 360-degree loop-de-loop, and Gus wanted a repeat. I looked over at Sumner. He was obviously a skilled pilot and had a kind of swagger that made his suggestion a tempting invitation to adventure.

"Sure. Go for it, Sumner," I said, hunkering down and trying not to seem nervous.

"Aaaagh!" we screamed in unison as the centrifugal force of the maneuver pinned us to our seats. We were all laughing with relief as the plane righted itself and Sumner pointed at the tundra below.

"Lookee there!"

"What? I don't see anything," I said, scanning the terrain that was zooming by.

"Down there. See 'em runnin'?" Barely visible from our height was what appeared to be a herd of caribou on the move. "Let's go down for a better view," Sumner said, nosing the plane downward. I knew from having taken flying lessons that safety regulations dictated that a pilot should never take a plane below five hundred feet unless he has a landing site. If the engine cuts out, you're screwed. That minor technicality was not a deterrent to Sumner, a free spirit, who seemed more at home in the skies than on solid ground. He banked the plane twice and maneuvered within a couple hundred feet of the pack, continuing to drop altitude.

"How close are you gonna get, Sumner?"

"I like to be able to tell the males from the females," Sumner said, giving me a rakish smile like a coolly confident Hans Solo grinning at a frightened Chewbacca. At about fifty feet above the racing hoofs, Sumner leveled out. Man, what a sight it was gliding over the wild herd. I was still watching the thundering crush of caribou out the side window when I noticed a shotgun strapped to the rear of the plane.

"Whadda use that for?" I asked, nodding to the gun.

"Just in case I have to put an injured passenger out of his misery."

My head swiveled toward him.

"Ha, ha . . . just jokin' with ya. 'Course, ya never know. There're bears down there."

"Yeah, but we're up here."

"Fur the time bein'."

"I guess this can be a pretty dangerous job."

"Not as dangerous as my last one."

I had to ask, "What was that?"

"Used to mule marijuana from Mexico in this buggy. Gettin' too old for that now," he sighed. "Too risky nowadays!" I wondered whether it was riskier than flying up the butts of racing caribou, but I kept my thoughts to myself.

George's ploy worked. I was stoked on Alaska, and as soon as I returned home from the trip, I described it in glowing terms to the band. Just to sweeten the deal, I promised them an added vacation week in Hawaii. They played the Alaska gig and then flew directly to the sunny beaches of Maui. What a great way to kick off the summer!

# High Notes

About a year after our visit, I heard the sad news that Sumner had died in a plane crash. He'd been scouting film locations with Federico De Laurentis, the son of Dino De Laurentis, the film producer, when his plane and another collided in mid-air, killing everyone. I like to think that somewhere up in the wild blue yonder Sumner is trailing a host of angels, trying to tell the males from the females.

# CHAPTER 23

## STILL TRUCKIN'

It's curious that men tend to forget or ignore anniversaries; maybe they're just not sentimental by nature.

June 1980 would have come and gone with no one the wiser and no acknowledgement of the day in 1965 when Phil Lesh joined the Warlocks, officially forming the Grateful Dead, were it not for Colorado promoter Barry Fey. He knew the value of the anniversary connection and booked shows in Boulder on June 6 and 7, using the anniversary connection to boost ticket sales.

Barry's reminder set Bill Graham in motion too. Bill loved a good party, especially when a special occasion could increase the take at the turnstiles. He took out a full-page ad in the *San Francisco Chronicle* and plastered the page with his famous quote: "They are not the best at what they do; they are the only ones who do what they do." His epigrammatic quote had become so familiar that the Deadheads instantly recognized it, even though the ad made no mention of the Grateful Dead. Fans embraced its esoteric appeal and Bill's fifteenth-anniversary Grateful Dead shows in September and October sold out in record time.

He felt deeply connected to the band and took great pains to make the run a special one. He installed speakers in the lobby so fans could dance there as well as in the auditorium. Memorabilia from the band's fifteen years together competed for wall space in the lobby, and a gorgeous poster depicting the Warfield Theater with two huge skeletons wearing Uncle Sam hats was on prominent display and for sale. Balloons were everywhere, a relaxed party mood prevailed, and the smell of marijuana wafted through the air. When the band returned to the stage for their final encore on the last night, they found a table with champagne on ice and a row of glasses. Jerry raised his glass in celebration, and a spotlight lit up the audience, revealing each fan holding a glass and toasting the band.

## Party at Radio City Music Hall

When the dates had been set for the Warfield shows, I called John Scher in New Jersey and said, "Listen, John, Graham is going all-out on these fifteenth-anniversary shows. Can we come up with some equally impressive spectacle in New York?"

John paused for a second and said, "It's a long shot, but we might be able to get into Radio City Music Hall."

"Get out! They only play G-rated films. The management will never allow a bunch of freaks in there!"

"I think they might. They're trying to hang onto the place," John continued. "They went bankrupt and the place was nearly demolished. It's just been restored and they need money to keep it going. In fact, attempts were made to convert the building into office spaces. John Belushi delivered an irate commentary on *Saturday Night Live*'s Weekend Update segment, and because of that, the public outcry, and the commercial interests, the place has been preserved as a New York City landmark."

"Check it out and let me know. I won't mention a word to anyone. Christ, we could do a week there, no problem. Let 'em know we're serious and how much money they can make. What a coup if we can pull that off!"

"I'm on it!" John said and hung up. He called back in short order with the good news that the top brass at Radio City had agreed to allow us to grace their hallowed hall. A year earlier, the idea of the Grateful Dead playing Radio City Music Hall would have been unthinkable to the conservative management. We booked eight concerts over ten days, ending on Halloween night. They would be the first performances by a rock band in Radio City Music Hall's history.

This occasion had to be documented. John set up a meeting with Jerry and his respected Capitol Theater videographer, Len Dell'Amico. He was a good match and plans began for a concert documentary; Len would direct it and I would produce it. Six cameras were set up surrounding the stage with a thirty-track, in-synch audio recording system. The audio and video would be edited and mixed afterwards. The finished products, the *Dead Reckoning* record and the *Dead Ahead* video, were marketed by Arista Records and Monterey Video and became collectors' items.

John and I knew the concerts would sell out in record time and, despite the six-thousand-seat capacity of the Music Hall, many fans would be left out of the celebration. To include fans outside the metropolitan area, we did a simulcast of the Halloween show on the final night via closed-circuit TV to twenty theaters with full concert sound as far west as Chicago and as far south as Florida. The multi-state theater concert video event, the first of its kind, gave thousands of loyal Deadheads a unique Halloween treat.

Al Franken and Tom Davis, writer-comedians from *Saturday Night Live* and friends of the band since the Dead had been guests on the show, hosted the event. As Brent Mydland introduced them to the packed Radio City Music Hall crowd, he joked, "I don't know who these guys are, but they're not very funny. Ladies and gentlemen, Frank and Dave." Al and Tom added their unique brand of wry and self-satirizing humor to the proceedings and were a welcomed addition to the shows.

## Culture Clash

Part of the fun for concertgoing Deadheads is waiting in long lines, meeting new, like-minded free spirits, and getting high on marijuana and on each other. To these loyal folks, a Grateful Dead concert was not only about the music; it was a ritual of celebration, a ceremonial coming together of friends to revel in the party atmosphere of the event. With this mindset, more than two thousand fans with an ocean of patience waited in line, many camping out for three days on the sidewalk for the opportunity to snag one of the fifty thousand tickets.

The Dead play radically different sets each night, and many zealous fans buy tickets for multiple performances. It's not unusual for a thousand or more fans from around the country to follow the band on their tours and attend multiple shows in multiple cities. By 1980, Dead fans were of all ages: Parents who were young fans in the early days brought their children; older kids brought younger siblings; there were young fans, old fans, and fans of all ages in between. Deadheads often got a bad rap as hippies, but most of the hard-edged criticism came from those outside the scene who were jealous of the happy, free-spirited existence they could only observe. The day of the first concert, John and I arrived early to check out the crowd gathering before the show. The ticket line was five blocks long and so wide it was spilling into the streets of New York, incurring the wrath of motorists.

"Hey ya fuckin' little freak, get outta the street!" a cabbie screamed. "We're tryin' to drive here!"

"Oh, sorry, dude," the skinny ponytailed kid answered, pushing back into the crowd.

In defense of their fellow Deadhead, others in line shouted, "Cool it, man." "You need to smoke a little dope." "Peace, brother."

The furious cabbie yelled back, "I'll give ya peace—a piece of my fuckin' fist!" The crowd of excited concertgoers complied as best they could, and most of the passing New Yorkers chuckled at the gypsies who had temporarily taken over their streets. Overall the crowd was peaceful, cheering for TV cameras that arrived to film the goings-on and joking with reporters, jubilant in the knowledge that before long they'd have their precious tickets. It was a joy to witness the prevailing sense of camaraderie among Grateful Dead devotees.

John and I were enjoying the interaction when one of the stage crew came running up. "Richard, the suits are going crazy. You gotta talk to 'em."

It was nearly showtime when John and I walked into the executive offices of Radio City Music Hall; the room was filled with grim-faced, middle-aged men. The Music Hall's chief administrator, flanked by his legal counsel, approached us and said, "We are canceling the show."

The lawyers appeared to be serious but were clearly just grandstanding for the benefit of their clients. I knew they didn't have a legal leg to stand on. We had the signed contracts.

"On what grounds?" I asked.

"This is a historic site and we won't have it desecrated."

"We don't want it desecrated either. What specifically are we talking about?"

"Those garish skeleton posters in the lobby, ridiculing our recent financial problems."

He was referring to the skeletons in Uncle Sam hats on the commemorative posters framing the Radio City Music Hall's marquee. For years, the Dead had used skeletal figures in various kinds of dress to celebrate band festivities. The skeletons were a reference to both the band's name and the Mexican Day of the Dead figures, which symbolize the precious and tenuous nature of life. The Radio City Music Hall staff had mistakenly interpreted them as a satire on the near demise of their beloved institution. I tried to explain but to no avail. Finally, to appease them and save the eight-show run, we agreed to rescind sales of the poster. I left the meeting and descended the stairs into the lobby, wondering if relations between generations would always be marked by such misunderstanding and hostility.

The lobby was filling with colorfully dressed Deadheads, many with long flowing hair and beards. I spotted a dignified, elderly man whose urbane appearance in a hat, suit, tie, and overcoat was conspicuous in the denim-clad throng. One blown-away Deadhead stopped to stare and asked, "What're you doing here, man? You like this music?"

The man stopped, turned, and replied with great courtesy, "Young man, the Grateful Dead is the greatest rock 'n' roll band ever!"

The Deadhead shook the old man's hand and exclaimed, "Gee, I wish my grandfather was like you!"

I caught up to the elderly gentleman and gently seized his arm. When he turned, I said, "Dad, I'm so glad you made it!"

"Richard," my father said, embracing me, "I wouldn't miss it for the world!"

In truth, my father's attendance at a Dead concert was a once-in-a-lifetime event. He was a big Sinatra fan and a classically trained musician. His presence seemed a good omen for the future of Radio City Music Hall, signaling openness to the new while honoring the old. The Dead concerts were a financial success and paved the way for other groups in subsequent years. I like to think we ushered in an era of relevance and prosperity for this revered civic institution and helped to ease the transition of musical tastes from one generation to another.

# PART FOUR:

# THE GRATEFUL DEAD MERRY-GO-ROUND

*Germany, Mississippi River Boat, Watch the River Flow, Sirens of Titan, and Garcia-Grisman*

# CHAPTER 24

# FROM DEUTSCHLAND TO THE SOUTH LAND

"Wake up asshole! Open the fuckin' door!" I was jolted out of a deep sleep by the loud demands of someone pounding on my hotel door.

It was five o'clock in the morning March 29, 1981, in Essen Germany and the Dead and The Who had played a double bill show the night before at the Rockpalast concert hall. I was exhausted after the show and bowed out of the after-concert celebration in the hotel bar earlier than most, leaving The Who and Dead band members and some of the crew to party late into the night.

I sat up abruptly, not fully awake, and tried to clear my head. Was it a fire? Was it a bust? Did someone overdose? I staggered out of bed and opened the door. Wham! Bill Kreutzmann slammed me against the wall, pinning me with his forearm pressed into my throat. I was definitely awake then, but I couldn't breathe. Kreutzmann's eyes were wild with cocaine-fueled anger, and his face was flushed with booze. "You lying, thieving piece a shit! You've been stealing from us!" In a flash I realized he'd been up all night and was now crazy and paranoid. "You're fired!" he screamed in a rage.

"Okay! Okay!" I gasped. "Let go!" He released me, turned, and bolted out the door as suddenly as he'd arrived. It wasn't the wakeup call I'd been expecting, but one thing was for sure—there was no going back to sleep. It was déjà vu all over again. Kreutzmann had done almost the same thing to Jon McIntire on the drug-fueled

European tour back in 1974, and it seemed as if nothing had changed. I knew I had done a good job of streamlining operations and keeping the cash flow steady, but it was getting harder to deal with the grind of tours, the bullshit, and the fucked up, out-of-control behavior. In the old days, I would have talked to Jerry about it, but he was so consumed by his addiction I no longer felt I had the same empathetic friend to confide in.

I checked out of the hotel, headed to Paris, and spent some solitary time contemplating what had happened and what I wanted to do with my future. Kreutzmann was a loose cannon with others too. In Phil Lesh's memoir, *Searching for the Sound,* he recounts an incident with Bill; when Phil responded to Bill's announcement about firing me with, "Well that was a stupid move!" Kreutzmann grabbed him by the neck in a burst of uncontrolled anger. Reflecting on the incident, Phil was quoted as saying, "I was not happy with the departure of one of the best managers we'd had." At the time, I wasn't exactly sure what was going on with the other band members, but it was clear Phil was not pleased with Bill.

Shortly after I returned to California, Kreutzmann paid me a visit, apologized, and assured me I had the band's complete support. For me, the incident in the hotel room marked a change in my relationship with the band. I'd had it and it was time for me to move on. I worked for them a little longer in a reduced capacity but turned the day-to-day operations over to Danny Rifkin, a trusted and competent professional. I began investigating the possibilities of producing more creative ventures and events for the Dead. It was a temporary work solution, but it let me get out from under the stress and still allowed me to retain my connection to the band. I dreamed of taking them to other exotic locations as I had done in Egypt and

Alaska—places where they could make history as well as music—but I needed Jerry's support and he was lost in another phase of his personal odyssey. He was no longer living in idyllic Stinson Beach with Mountain Girl. He was holed up in Rock Scully's basement, where he was well supplied with whatever he needed for his visits to dreamland. He was no longer interested in the kind of adventures I envisioned. He was taking his own personal trips to other places. Amazingly, he did some of his best artwork during this period, bringing back memorable images from his private sojourns and applying them to canvas and other graphic media with stunning results. Life takes us on different journeys, and Jerry and I were no longer on the same path.

## Roll On, Big River

On a beautiful October morning in 1980, during a walk along the mighty Mississippi River, I'd been struck by a creative inspiration. I was in New Orleans with the Dead for a couple of sold-out shows at the venerable Saenger Theatre before heading to New York for the anniversary concerts, and I was up and out at sunrise enjoying the peace and quiet. Taking in the majesty, grace, and power of the river spilling over its banks as the steamboat *Natchez* chugged along a few feet away from me, I visualized the band doing a weeklong riverboat tour tracing the rich musical heritage that had sprung from the river's banks.

We would start with a concert in St. Paul, Minnesota, and work our way south, doing additional shows in the riverfront cities of St. Louis and Memphis and ending with an outdoor blowout musical extravaganza in New Orleans. There would be mini concerts on the riverboat stage with the Dead and guest artists such as David

Grisman, Garcia's banjo mentor Ralph Stanley, and John Hartford, who would play fiddle and banjo, sing, and share his extensive knowledge of Mississippi River lore. Mickey could introduce Hamza El Din, the Egyptian oudist who'd played with the Dead in Egypt, as an example of a musician from another culture who was equally inspired by a mighty river, in his case, the mighty Nile. The musical-cultural possibilities were limitless. The cost would be covered by Deadheads wanting passage on the boat with the band, concerts along the way, at least a two-record set, and profits from a documentary film.

My idea was hugely ambitious, and I had too many things on my plate at the time to seriously pursue it. Now, with Danny covering the Dead's daily operations, I had the freedom and energy to devote to the project. I told the band I had a great special event idea that involved the Mississippi River and would have a proposal for them by the end of May. Randy Sarti and I flew to the Big Easy and took a tour on the *Mississippi Queen*, a beautiful charter riverboat, with facilities for four hundred passengers and a three-hundred-seat theater. The project was not only possible but also had the potential of earning a lot of money in a variety of ways.

## Troubled Waters

When the day came to pitch the project at a band meeting, I was prepared and excited. Jerry was late getting there and arrived in a dark mood. I hoped my presentation would spark his enthusiasm. I passed around photos of the *Mississippi Queen*, outlined the prospective concert sites in New Orleans and along the river, and suggested possible themes and guests. I ended the presentation with a sound financial plan that I hoped would seal the deal. When I opened the subject for discussion, Jerry spoke up immediately, "Nah, we don't want to do that."

No one said a word. Dead silence. When Jerry axed the project, no one asked for further discussion or questioned his decision. I knew Mickey and Bob were excited about the proposal, but if Jerry wasn't in, nobody was. Jerry held absolute sway over the Grateful Dead. Sometimes that worked in my favor. This time, however, his decision crushed not only the idea but also my hopes of taking the Dead in new directions with fun, creative potential. Deflated and exasperated, I told Jerry a month or so later that it was time for me to quit the Dead scene. We still had ties involving several film projects and Danny knew I was available if he needed me, but I was out the door. The Grateful Dead was more than a band; it was a cultural institution. And like all institutions, it offered compensation and security but at a price. It was a price I was no longer willing to pay.

## The River Flows on Like a Breath

Even though the Mississippi River tour had not worked out, I felt that the river as a cradle for contemporary American music was a fascinating topic. I liked the title *Watch the River Flow,* and I thought of combining original footage of great rock 'n' roll and classic blues musicians in concert with historical images of the old and new South. I wanted to cinematically tell the story of the evolution of rock, jazz, and blues from their origins in Delta music—slavery, field hollers, work crews, and juke joints—to the popular forms we enjoy today. The film would inform primarily through music. I had the vision, and now I needed to figure out a way to make it work.

Through mutual friends in New York City, I had met a talented young writer, Warren Leight, and he agreed to co-write a "Watch the

River Flow" screenplay. We were a good team and became good friends. He was a native New Yorker in his early twenties and a recent Stanford School of Journalism grad. I had New York roots, was in my late thirties, and was a recent "school of Grateful Dead" grad. We both had shoulder-length hair that we knew wouldn't ingratiate us in the South, so we cut our locks and drove south to New Orleans.

## Every Day I Sing the Blues

The Tigress Club, a dilapidated clapboard building that in a former life had served as a Veterans of Foreign Wars hall, was on the wrong side of the tracks. Canton, Mississippi, was a small town and many storefronts in the neighborhood around the club were boarded up. An exception was the liquor store, whose windows were full of ads for malt beer, cheap wine, and Kool cigarettes. We learned by chance of a show at the Tigress and wanted to check it out. As we neared the entrance of the club, a black man in a colorful sport coat motioned to me. I had no idea what he wanted, but I walked over to him with cautious curiosity.

"Say, my man, you gonna need some juice inside!" he said.

"Juice?"

"Bourbon, brother!" he smiled. "Y'all wanna loosen up a little, right?"

"Yeah, sure, I guess."

"Well, they don't sell no hooch inside. Ain't got no liquor license." He slipped a bottle of what he was calling bourbon out of a nearby cardboard box, dropped it in a brown paper bag, and handed it to me. I looked around and slipped him a ten, trying to look as nonchalant as I had in my old drug-scoring days.

"All right, my man, enjoy the show!"

Inside was smoky and dim, and the air was heavily fragrant with sweet perfume mingling with the savory aroma of soul food. A portable stage and dance floor were at one end; at the other was the kitchen, where waitresses emerged carrying paper plates loaded with barbecued ribs, fried chicken, and heaps of slaw. Warren and I made our way to a small table close to the front of the stage, and a smiling waitress in a tight, red skirt brought us a "setup" consisting of a bucket of ice and glasses. We were the only white guys in the room. I took out my bottle of hooch and poured Warren and myself a double; we both needed to loosen up. Bourbon or whatever, it sure as hell hit the spot!

The shabby décor didn't stop the crowd from dressing in their snappy best. Men sported shiny suits with pressed white shirts, and women were done up in bright dresses and high, high heels. Everyone was wearing the look that said *this* was a special night. By the time the band took the stage to warm up the crowd, Warren and I were already feeling warm ourselves from the juice, and we relaxed into the opening riff of a drummer, bass player, keyboardist, and two horn players. At the end of a couple of tunes, a big black man in a tuxedo stepped up to the microphone and announced, "Ladies and gentlemen, the King of the Blues, Mr. B.B. King!"

Man! The crowd went crazy! They couldn't have been more excited if he'd introduced Jesus. Women screamed and stretched out their hands towards the husky, smiling B.B. King as he took the stage. Men shouted and clapped.

B.B. started with a short version of "Every Day I Sing the Blues" and then rapped to the audience about how he'd grown up in Mississippi, as many blues legends had. He explained how the music had been around there a long time, way back to when the black folks sang in the fields to get the work done. The crowd cheered and the women were just short of hysterical as he told his story. "Back in forty-nine, I was a deejay, and every record I played—well, I was as good as the guys on the recording. I started singing and playing—done it ever since."

Warren and I turned to each other in disbelief. This was the story we had come to hear—the living history of the Mississippi's music. It was a mythic treasure, and we were thrilled to share in the musical riches.

## The Fickle Hand of Fate

After the amazing trip, we both started researching, organizing, and developing ideas for a film script. We kept *Watch the River Flow* as a working title and decided to divide the film into three parts: Arrival, Migration, and Emigration. The Arrival segment would be a concert featuring Randy Newman, Eric Clapton, Howlin' Wolf, Ray Charles, and maybe other artists, interspersed with the story of African slaves, the origins of Delta music, historical photos, and archival footage. The second segment, Migration, would depict the movement of the music out of the South to the North, especially Chicago, with clips of Muddy Waters, Bo Diddley, and Elvis. Emigration, the third segment, would describe how the music spread to Europe and returned via groups such as The Beatles and Stones, and other performers, including Eric Clapton.

We felt confident about the script and the concept, so we focused on financing. The project needed to be attached to a name with clout to attract money and musical artists. Jerry was just that guy, and he was my first option because of his love for film, his experience in directing and editing, and the appeal the music held for him. I had reservations about asking him but decided to pitch him anyway. He liked the idea and agreed to let me use his name to solicit backing. Although it looked like he was going to rally, he continued to grow more lethargic and wasn't able to contribute any real energy to the project.

Even with Jerry's name, I couldn't induce other bankable celebrities to come aboard for a variety of reasons. Some were committed to other projects, others were dealing with personal problems, and so it went. As a last resort, I managed to get Jerry to go along with me to see Bill Graham. Bill thought the project had merit but begged off, saying he had a full schedule. I think he sensed Jerry's lack of energy, and he wasn't going to do me any favors due to our contentious history.

Try as we did, we just couldn't get the necessary backing. I was deeply disappointed that this worthwhile project wasn't going to happen. During my years in the business, I had learned that a successful movie, album, or concert often hinges on the fortuitous—the right time, place, and favorable coincidences—and none of those were in our favor. As one door closed behind me, I waited for another to open. That door turned out to be the Golden Gate Bridge. I left my old life behind and moved to San Francisco.

# CHAPTER 25

# FORTY-NINE SQUARE MILES SURROUNDED ENTIRELY BY REALITY

Paul Kantner's description of San Francisco is one of my favorites. The city *did* have an unreal quality about it—and for all the right reasons.

I was ready to embrace a big change in my life and the City by the Bay welcomed me with open arms. Deborah, my ever-supportive partner, found us new digs on the top of Russian Hill, looking out over the bay, with the hills of Marin from my past life in the distance. Finally off the Grateful Dead merry-go-round, I was looking forward to unwinding and spending quality time with myself, Deborah, and my eight-year-old son, Gus, who was coming to live with us in San Francisco, much to our delight.

Gus got to ride the cable car to his new school, the Cathedral School for Boys, on the top of Nob Hill. Deborah started working with the well-known entertainment attorney Michael Krassner in the Stadtmuller House law offices at 819 Eddy Street—a building whose walls strained to contain the larger-than-life personalities of Krassner, Michael Stepanian, Terrance Hallinan, and Brian Rohan. I quickly adopted the morning routine of a brisk, introspective walk down our hill to North Beach, San Francisco's Italian neighborhood, to soak up the European-like atmosphere and enjoy the cafés and the people. If I timed it just right, my favorite sidewalk table at the

## High Notes

Café Greco—where they served the best real Italian coffee—would be flooded with sunshine, creating an inviting and comfortable spot for me to happily wile away the morning hours watching the people pass by on Columbus Avenue and talking to other café-goers and my favorite barista, Michele Ruocca. Michele served his coffee with a twinkle, irrepressible Italian humor, and hospitality. He was never too busy to offer a big smile and an enthusiastic, sincere "Buon giorno!" Sitting down one morning, I heard his familiar voice.

"Ah, mio amico Riccardo! Buon giorno! Buon giorno!" Michele said, as he placed a perfectly foam-topped cappuccino in front of me.

"Buon giorno, Michele!"

"Ah, si, si! It is a good day! The sun is shining, the women are beautiful, and my best customer is here! What could be better?"

"Maybe if your best customer was a beautiful woman."

"Are you sure you're not from Capri?" Michele said with an ear-to-ear smile. Michele had grown up on the Isle of Capri, and his heart was always there. He spoke of his island and its people with a warm, endearing glow that made you want to go to that paradise. If he told you he thought you might be from Capri, you had earned his highest compliment. Over time, he and I became close friends. Deborah got to know him well too, and as luck would have it, we were able to visit him and his family on his beloved isle and share its beauty. Capri was all he said it was, and more.

Michele was typical of many of the people I met during this phase of my life—people with whom I connected not for business or expediency but simply for the pleasure of their company. The universe was giving me a chance to rejuvenate. Life was opening up in many wonderful and surprising ways, and I was savoring every moment. Deborah and I took every opportunity to explore the city—visiting its many cafés, shops, neighborhoods, theaters, and museums, excitedly sharing our discoveries with Gus. Like so many before us, we fell in love with San Francisco, with all its scenic charms and cultural diversity.

## Would You Like a Side of Porn with Your Order?

The city had always had a great film culture, and by the late 70s and early 80s, a score of art-house theaters, film institutes, and museum programs offered filmgoers the chance to not only see classic films but also learn about the history and heritage of the movies. A large group of dedicated cinephiles were interested and supportive attendees of the many venues all over the city. In the early 80s, the fast-growing availability and popularity of VHS recorders and movies on tape started a noticeable shift in where viewers were watching their movies. Film buffs didn't abandon the city's cinematic houses, but they started watching many more movies at home. VHS and Beta formats were cutting-edge at the time and a major innovation that changed both the culture and commerce of movies.

I was fascinated with the breakthrough technology and started kicking around some ideas about ways I might be able to combine my love of classic film and a viable commercial venture. I considered opening a video store specializing in classic, art, and specialty films and staffing it with an informed crew of local film buffs and scholars, but the neighborhoods were suddenly overrun with big corporate video store operations. I could see that a small specialty video shop would have problems with inventory and overhead. On a weekend getaway to a small resort in the wine country north of San Francisco, it occurred to me that these small, trendy, upscale properties would be the perfect place to market a visual amenity. The resort guests could choose a quality movie from a specially selected menu of feature films and watch it in the relaxed comfort of their rooms. Watching a movie would be the perfect way to end a day of wine tasting and fine dining, especially considering that the properties I was considering were in rural areas with essentially no other nightlife. I chose the name Room Service Theatre and started developing my idea.

I ran the specs by my travel agent friend from the old Dead days, Randy Sarti, who thought that the idea had great potential as a business venture and partnered up. We put together a financial plan, recruited some investors, made some sales presentations, and before you could say "action," Room Service Theatre was in business. Our first clients were in northern California, but over time we added out-of-state clients as well. At first, we focused on providing a select variety of high-quality feature films and a smattering of children's films to entertain the kids when their parents wanted to relax.

To our surprise, before long the resorts started relaying guest requests for adult films. We deliberated about including them in our selection and decided to give it a try. Most of the resort customers were adult couples, young and old. In the 80s, porn viewing was transitioning from the taboo to the mainstream, although our viewers liked their privacy. In a few properties, we introduced a small selection of what we considered to be the least offensive, best-produced erotica we could find, and it wasn't long before rental receipts showed not Chaplin, Wells, and Hitchcock, but Linda Lovelace, Johnny Wadd, and Aunt Peg. With the popularity came many an amusing call from concierges.

"Hello, this is Edward from the Sonoma Mission Inn. They've stolen *Every Woman's Fantasy*—again! Can you send us another?"

"That's the third time this quarter!"

"Yes, it's a favorite."

"Did you charge the guest the replacement fee?"

"Yes, of course. They don't seem to care."

"Why do people pay a fifty-dollar replacement fee when they could go to the adult store and buy the same movie for twenty dollars?"

"I think they're too embarrassed to buy it in person. You know, it's kind of a touchy subject."

"Edward?"

"Yes, sir?"

"Are you putting me on?"

Room Service Theatre eventually fell victim to newer technologies when most of our properties switched to cable or on-demand services. We were lucky to have the run we did. Room Service Theatre provided us with a positive financial return, a great library of classic films, and some tasteful erotica.

# CHAPTER 26

## THE SAGA OF SIRENS

"Puny man can do nothing at all to help or please
God Almighty, and Luck is not the hand of God."
—Chief Teachings of the Church of God
the Utterly Indifferent
Kurt Vonnegut, *The Sirens of Titan*

A Bette Davis look-alike—large-eyed and middle-aged—opened the door and impatiently motioned for John Kahn and me to enter her elegant Upper West Side Manhattan apartment. It was Lucy Kroll, John's godmother and a well-connected New York talent agent.

Her place was tastefully decorated and had great views of the city, but before I had a chance to take it all in, Lucy dropped all semblance of a hostess demeanor and turned into a no-nonsense agent addressing the business at hand. "Are you really serious about wanting to secure the film rights to Vonnegut's book. What's it called again?"

"*The Sirens of Titan,*" I replied.

Jerry, John, and I started our quest to make a movie of Vonnegut's novel in 1977. With steady regularity, Jerry and I had been watching movies from a wide variety of genres in our Mill Valley office, using a projector and a roll-down screen. At that time, Jerry was steeped in his love for movies and bursting with boundless, creative energy. One morning, John popped in and we shared our amazement at the artistic and box office success of the recently released Spielberg film *Close Encounters of the Third Kind.* The conversation turned to one of Jerry's all-time favorite novels, Kurt Vonnegut's *The Sirens of Titan.* It was a favorite of John's and mine as well. We all shared a deep appreciation for Vonnegut's wonderfully wry and sardonic sci-fi classic, and our imaginations ran wild with what it would be like as a film.

"Man! Wouldn't it be far out to make that?" Jerry said. The conversation continued, and in our enthusiasm, we started to fantasize about the possibility of doing the project ourselves or at least spearheading it. I knew that working on an endeavor like that would bring out the film genius in Jerry and thought he just might have the clout to attract the financing.

"Why don't I see if the rights are available?" I suggested, planting the seed. "If they're not outrageously priced, we can option them and see if we can get a development deal."

John jumped to life, "My godmother in New York is a literary agent. I can give her a call!"

Jerry's face lit up. "Far fuckin' out! Let's do it!"

Now John and I were in New York representing ourselves and Jerry, who wanted to direct the film. Facing the formidable Lucy Kroll, we felt a little bit like a couple of mischievous trick-or-treaters who had finagled our way into the literary candy store.

"No fooling around here!" Lucy cautioned. "If I call Vonnegut's legal representative and it's available, we have to follow through. After all, I have a reputation to uphold." Lucy's reputation wasn't my main concern, especially when she added, "You'll need a literary attorney, and I only work with the best, of course!" Of course. And the best would mean a big legal fee, and 10 percent to Lucy, plus whatever we'd have to pay Vonnegut.

The rights were available, and we optioned the book for six years, for sixty thousand dollars.

John and I worked on a treatment and a scene-by-scene literal adaptation of the book in screenplay format. Jerry liked the story and didn't want to change it much, so we didn't. I knew it was going to be a tough sell to the studios. Jerry had no directorial experience, and studios don't throw millions of dollars into a film on a lark. However, I was hoping that Jerry's influence could attract a big Hollywood name and secure the services of a veteran assistant director or cinematographer to handle the technical side.

## Stranded, Saved, and Shelved

Like Vonnegut's characters on the remote moon Titan, the project languished for years, stranded by our demanding schedules, the difficulty of getting studio backing, and plain old human procrastination.

In 1983, a year or so after I resigned from the Grateful Dead, I had the time and energy to get back to work on the Vonnegut project and asked Warren Leight, who had done such a great job for me on the Mississippi River project, to adapt the book for the screen. True to form, Warren's script was spot-on, and I couldn't wait to give it to Jerry. I hoped he'd read it right away and that the great job Warren had done would renew his interest and reignite the spark. However, we barely got a response from Jerry. He was sliding into his own private fantasy drug world, and it was only through my persistence that we heard anything at all.

Word of the project reached *Saturday Night Live* actor and staff writer Tom Davis, who was doing some pretty heavy drug partying with Jerry, which gave him access to Jerry that Warren and I didn't have. Tom used his connections to get the novel to Bill Murray, who had the potential for being the star to move the project forward. Murray was riding high on the recent success of *Ghostbusters*, and the studios were anxious to bankroll his project of choice. Bill read the book, loved it, and wanted to play the role of Malachi Constant, the novel's protagonist. Things spun somewhat out of control, and Davis overshadowed Warren, despite my strong suggestion to Jerry that he look at Warren's superlative screenplay again.

With Murray's commitment and the revived interest, I got pulled back into the fray and ended up in LA at a meeting with super-agent Michael Ovitz, Jerry, Tom, Bill, and Gary Gutierrez—the special effects artist whose company had been creating visuals for the film. I expected a meeting with big-name movie and music stars and high-powered Hollywood movers and shakers about a possible multi-million-dollar film project to be a serious affair. I was wrong. While Ovitz and I, the business guys, were at one end of a huge table talking about financing, development, and rights, Bill was at the other end playing the role of a billiard pocket. His mouth was wide open at the edge of the table, waiting while Tom attempted to roll gumballs across the hardwood into his mouth.

Despite his shenanigans, Bill had serious Hollywood juice, and based on his interest alone, Ovitz was able to get us a development deal at Universal Pictures with an advance of two hundred fifty thousand dollars. It covered the cost of the book rights, an option renewal, full storyboards, drawings, paintings, incidentals, and Tom's draft of the screenplay. Warren Leight's original masterpiece of a screenplay was not only ignored but never even acknowledged. Tom's desperate desire to bond with Jerry and his drug-fueled insensitivity dealt a nasty blow to Warren, and to me. I never fully got over it, but my consolation was that Warren went on to win a Tony Award for his play *Sideman,* finally getting the recognition for his writing that he deserved.

Bill Murray took a stab at shedding his droll clown character by playing a dramatic role in the big-budget remake of Somerset Maugham's *The Razor's Edge,* a novel of spiritual transformation. The film was a commercial flop, and Bill, stung by harsh reviews, moved to Europe and sidelined himself for several years. Without his involvement, Universal shelved the project.

I made one big last effort to renew the venture. I sent a copy of the book and screenplay to the well-known director Jonathan Demme, who was in New York making *Married to the Mob.* The idea of Sirens intrigued him, and I set up a meeting, on location. Jerry was too enervated by then to muster enough energy and enthusiasm to interest Demme, and Demme was distracted by problems he was having on the set of his film, so the meeting went nowhere. That was the final, disappointing end of *The Sirens of Titan* for me.

Somewhere in the universe, I'm sure someone is trying to make that wonderful novel into a film, but I fear it could be a millennium before Malachi Constant leaves the dimension of the printed page and materializes on the silver screen. As Vonnegut himself cryptically wrote, "And so it goes."

# CHAPTER 27

## FAREWELL TO A FRIEND

I first met Jerry Garcia back in the fall of 1970 in New York, when David Grisman took me backstage at the Fillmore East. He had suggested that I move to California, and I eventually became Jerry's personal manager, and then an agent and manager for the Grateful Dead. Even when I worked for the Dead, I continued to handle Jerry's personal affairs outside the Dead. We had a long and involved professional relationship for over twenty years and were also close personal friends.

I admired and supported him, and he reciprocated with his friendship, his trust, and the power of his influence. We shared many a happy hour together—hanging out, talking, listening to music, watching movies, and solving the world's problems. He had boundless depth, talent, and energy, and I enjoyed finding projects that ignited his interest. Sharing his enthusiasm was a joy.

Over the years, he'd done his share of drugs, but none got a hold of him like heroin. And when it did, much to my heartbreak, we drifted apart. By the mid-80s, he had a major dependence and had become more and more reclusive. He had little energy, was not interested in much, and didn't want to be disturbed. His condition attracted an odd assortment of people—most of whom didn't have his best interests at heart and enabled his increased isolation by deciding who could see him.

In 1986, Jerry suffered a diabetic coma for five days. When he came out of it, he was unable to play music due to physical and mental difficulties. Working hard to regain his skills, he made a quick recovery. Barely missing a beat, he hit the road with a grueling schedule that continued nonstop into the next year, leaving him exhausted. After the failed *Sirens of Titan* meeting with Jonathan Demme in New York in 1987, I didn't push for his involvement in anything, hoping that he'd get some-much needed rest and take care of himself.

After I resigned as manager for the Dead, I wasn't allowed backstage to visit with or speak to Jerry. On the Dead scene, you were either in or out—and I was definitely out. I was deeply concerned about Jerry's health. From afar it seemed at times that his needs were sacrificed for propping up the golden calf. Who knows? Human nature and motives are complex, and the Dead were no longer my world.

## Renewed Hope

Even though I was no longer in the business, my love for music was unabated. David had started his own label, Acoustic Disc, and his house and studio were always full of musicians recording or jamming, hanging out, getting high, and having fun. I had kept in touch with David Grisman over the years and enjoyed visiting him in his Mill Valley home and studio.

David too had been distanced from Jerry but for different reasons. Back in the Old and in the Way days, there had been a misunderstanding about work that David had performed for Round Records, and he was not fairly compensated. During that time, Round Records was owned by Jerry and Ron Rakow. Jerry had trusted Ron with the label's finances and was unaware that his friend had not been paid. The situation went unnoticed and unresolved for too long.

In 1990, David and Jerry ran into each other serendipitously at a San Francisco recording session. For reasons known only to Jerry, their reunion that night spurred him to authorize the Rex Foundation—a charity funded by the Grateful Dead—to honor David with its Ralph J. Gleason Award for his contribution to music, which was accompanied by a check for ten thousand dollars.

David invited Jerry to his home to sit in and play with his talented circle of musicians. Once again, the ol' pickin' pals were back playing the music they loved before a small group of family and friends, and Jerry was out and about again by himself.

## Peace Like a River Flows

"Hey, I got one for ya!" Jerry smiled, leaning over his guitar and coaxing out the plaintive melody. Like a spell, the music filled the small room, and Tony Rice, a southern bluegrass guitar virtuoso, started filling the spaces with impeccable riffs while David layered the mood with his tremulous mandolin. The old gospel, folk, and mountain tunes came to life with a timeless grace and beauty.

"I am a man of constant sorrow," Jerry intoned, closing his eyes while his honey and gravel voice rolled out a sad, sweet air that added to the reverie of those who played and those who listened.

Jerry tossed back his head. "Tony! Man! It's great playing with you!"

"Likewise!"

"We gotta do this more often!" David said.

"We will! We will!" Jerry promised. "I just got so many things goin' on, but we'll get it done!"

*The Grateful Dawg* documentary film, made by Gillian Grisman, and *The Pizza Tapes* CD, on David's Acoustic Disc label, feature David and Jerry and capture Jerry and his music during this latter creative period in his life.

To be with Jerry and David again and share in the camaraderie of their music and friendship held a special meaning for me. I felt in those last few encounters that I achieved closure in my relationship with my treasured friend and with my life in the music business.

I never saw Jerry again after 1993. He died of a heart attack at Serenity Knolls rehabilitation center in northern California in August 1995, at the age of fifty-three. Drugs, stress, an unhealthy lifestyle, and diabetes contributed, but in the end, that big heart had just worn out its body.

> "Now that the singer is gone, where
> shall I go for the song?"

> Robert Hunter, Jerry's longtime songwriting partner,
> wrote those words as part of his eulogy to Jerry.

Without Jerry, there was no Grateful Dead. The band members went their separate ways, and a unique chapter in American music closed.

As I read and talk about the stories here, I am reminded that many have been left out—not because they are any less significant but simply because the others were the ones that first popped into my old hippie brain.

I am grateful for *all* my experiences, for the privilege of being a part of it all, and for Alex Bushe's relentless and persistent encouragement to look in the rearview mirror.

# EPILOGUE

# GENES, FATE, AND LEGACY

## Music's Sweet Refrain

I grew up in a musically talented Italian-American family in which parents, siblings, aunts, uncles, cousins, and friends got together regularly to eat, drink, tease, joke, laugh, share music, and celebrate life in a wonderfully exuberant, gregarious Italian way. Music played a big part in our lives—there was *always* music and it bonded us and replenished our hearts and souls.

When I was a young boy, my grandparents lived a block away from us in New Jersey in a large, beautiful home with a spectacular view of New York City. It was a welcoming place for our family and friends and many evenings and Sundays found them hosting big, wonderful multicourse Italian dinners, followed by spirited musical performances.

At my young age of six or seven, those dinners made a huge impression on me and instilled a lifelong love and appreciation for the company of family and friends, fabulous cooking, stimulating and fun-filled conversation, and music. My Aunt Louisa sang Puccini and Verdi arias, my Aunt Tina played the piano, and my Dad played classical violin selections and sang heartfelt renditions of pop tunes and Italian folk favorites. Applause erupted after every selection, encouraging the music to continue late into the night. On more than one occasion, I snuck down after my bedtime and fell asleep hiding behind the statue at the foot of the stairs, listening to and absorbing my rich musical heritage.

When I was a little older, I was encouraged to continue the family tradition and take classical piano lessons. I wanted to embrace the piano, but my teacher had a no-nonsense, rigid, mechanical approach that stressed the discipline of learning over the joy, and the process was agonizing. I suffered through several years of her harsh instruction and became a technically competent but uninspired player. I could feel my love for music wilting, so I abandoned my formal musical training to preserve my passion for music. I switched my focus to obsessively attending live musical performances whenever I could to hear artists such as Maria Callas at the Metropolitan Opera House and Leonard Bernstein at Philharmonic Hall, often standing in line at the stage door afterwards for autographs. As a teenager in the burgeoning rock 'n' roll years of the 50s, I avidly listened to and followed the popular music artists of the era—Bill Haley, Buddy Holly, Chuck Berry, Elvis, and all the rest of the rockers, beboppers, and soul singers.

During the journey of living my life, I have always been curious about the many things that may or may not change our paths as we make our way: genes, fate, timing, luck, destiny, coincidence, synchronicity, a cosmic alignment of the stars, or maybe a host of illusive forces we can't even comprehend.

Looking back, I find myself flirting with the possibility that genes and fate, at least, might well have had something to do with my attraction to the music business and why I felt so comfortable and natural around musicians.

## Genes

Even though the classical training my parents had hoped to gift me with didn't take at the time, the strong musical gene I inherited is undeniable. I came from music, I love music of every genre, I need and seek out music, I find endless joy when listening to music, and I can't imagine a world without it. I am aware of other characteristics that I've inherited from my family. I share their perseverance and their strength to make the best of whatever surprises the universe has in store.

The American chapter of my family history began with my great-grandfather Giuseppe Giachino, who immigrated to New York from Turin, a town in Northern Italy, where distilling spirits was an art that had been perfected over centuries. Giuseppe studied and apprenticed with the masters, honing his proficiency at the highly specialized skill of distilling vermouth. When he arrived in America at the beginning of the century, however, there were no jobs in his field and he had to turn to a series of menial tasks.

By 1904, he had saved enough money to pay for his son Ferdinando, my grandfather, to leave Italy and join him in New York. They parlayed their old-world distilling skills and new-world economic opportunities into a flourishing winemaking business that catered to the city's burgeoning Italian community. The enterprise was so successful that my grandfather made a fortune in the hyped economy of the 1920s. He was able to return to Italy, where his profits allowed him to raise his family in the best traditions of European culture and elegance. His three children were educated in fine arts and classical music and lived a privileged life. The worldwide Great Depression at the end of the decade, however, devastated the family's finances and they were forced to return to New York.

Ferdinando labored hard and long to rebuild the business during the lean years of the Depression. His only son, my father Remo, who was a child prodigy on the violin and an honors graduate from the Music Conservatory in Turin, had to put his dreams of becoming a concert violinist aside to help in his father's struggle to resuscitate the family business. My father's two sisters, Tina and Louisa, who were also highly accomplished musicians, had to abandon their formal studies as well while the family tried to get back on its feet. Even though further education and careers in music were no longer viable for the three siblings, music remained an integral part of their lives.

The Depression shattered my Dad's dreams of a career in music, but it did not diminish his love of life. With an upbeat personality and an easygoing charm, he was a gifted salesman. If Arthur Miller's tragic *Death of a Salesman* had instead been the cheerful *Life of a Salesman,* he could have based it on my father. With the savoir faire of a streetwise Sinatra, he'd sing a song, tell a joke, and make a pitch that clients—mostly Italian restaurant owners—couldn't resist. His energy and optimism were infectious, and people loved being around him. In 1937, he met a beautiful Italian girl, Erminia, who worked in an office nearby in Greenwich Village. He began spending more time in her office than his own, and schmoozing became courting. Remo had saved his best pitch just for her. They were married in 1939, raised three sons, and had an amazing seventy-year union.

The family wine business, Vinvino, has been successful for five generations despite wars, hard times, and enormous cultural and technological changes. It continues to thrive in New York under the adept leadership of my brother Douglas and the efforts of my son, Gus, who both enjoy the rich inheritance of my Dad Remo's joie de vivre.

I too share my father's love for life, and just being with him—watching him and listening to him—strengthened our inherent bond and taught me how to interact with characters from all walks of life. As an agent in the competitive entertainment industry, I attribute my ability to cajole and persuade diverse individuals to watching and listening to my Dad. He didn't make sales—he made friends, and that is a quality I've always aspired to.

## Fate

During the summers of my high school years, I worked as a lifeguard and swim instructor at the posh Englewood Golf Club just outside Manhattan. My job exposed me to agents, promoters, celebrities, and their families. I had a taste of the glamour and excitement that was part of the showbiz lifestyle and was bitten by the bug. As fascinated as I was by their fast-paced and exciting world, I didn't think that it would ever be my world, so the dream faded and was replaced by others.

I set off to Gettysburg College, a small liberal arts school in Pennsylvania, and enrolled my freshman year as a biology major. I had decided to become a chiropractor and was excited and eager to start my studies. I had been introduced to the benefits of chiropracty through a family friend who was a chiropractor and a healer. He helped me rehabilitate after several injuries and mentored me in the art of holistic healing. I was impressed with his knowledge and ability to help people, with how the application extended beyond the science of medicine into the mysteries of nature, and with how it helped me.

However, my passion for becoming a chiropractor was abandoned when my love of showbiz was revived by a different kind of passion. I fell for a beautiful young actress in the theater department's performance of *South Pacific*. Smitten, I joined the Theater Arts Club and impulsively switched my major to English just to be around her. Our relationship was intense and short-lived, but connecting with theater and the arts more than compensated for my disappointment in love. While working on various school productions, I became friends with another student who was employed by a company that produced summer concerts, and he hired me as his assistant at their Baltimore venue. That next summer, after graduation, I returned to Baltimore as a theater manager. It was —as fate would have it—the beginning of my great adventure.

In retrospect, I see the hand of fortune in the breaks—both good and bad—that came my way. They tell the external story, but the deeper theme that formed my life is embodied in those evenings when that little boy fell asleep at the foot of the stairs as the music floated him away into melodious dreams.

## Legacy

I began meeting with Alex Bushe—the student from Bates College whose inquiries initiated this project in 2004—on a regular basis, and our conversations initially focused on the Egypt concerts. I considered them my crowning achievement, and those performances especially fascinated Alex. I gave him my video and audiotapes to edit and appointed him archivist for the Dead in Egypt.

As we investigated various project possibilities on the East Coast, history continued to unfold on the West Coast. Unbeknown to me, the remaining members of the Grateful Dead had turned over the contents of their audio-visual vault in San Rafael to Rhino Records and signed a ten-year agreement that gave Rhino exclusive rights to all their music and recordings.

Rhino had not only the rights to the music and recordings, but also my personal concert videotapes and my film of the Dead in Egypt, which I had stored in the vault. Working with Rhino proved to be a draining challenge. I wanted to make a full-length thirtieth-anniversary rockumentary, combining documentary and concert footage. My proposal alerted Rhino to the fact that they had something timely and of value to market, so they revisited the vaults, saw what they had, and wanted me to go away. After prolonged tribulations, negotiations, and compromises, Rhino finally and reluctantly allowed me to include fifteen minutes of my documentary footage as the "Vacation Tapes," a bonus on the DVD of the Dead's 2008 *Rocking the Cradle* DVD/CD package. The lack of cooperation from Rhino and the resulting abandonment of the more ambitious project were a big disappointment.

Alex did an outstanding job of editing, and I hope his work will be seen in its entirety someday. Meanwhile, the "Vacation Tapes" offer a glimpse of that unique chapter in the Grateful Dead history for fans to enjoy, and I am happy about that. I was impressed with Alex's energy and dedication to the project. During the consuming and challenging task of assembling and editing the endless footage for the "Vacation Tapes," I asked him how he had become interested in the Grateful Dead, given that he was so young when Jerry died and the Dead stopped playing.

Alex's answer was a soulful tribute to Jerry: "When I first heard Garcia play on a bootleg 1987 performance of the Dead doing 'All Along the Watchtower,' it was unlike anything I'd heard before. The sense of freedom and open-endedness in his playing really changed how I listened to and played music. After that, all I wanted to do was figure out how to play music with that kind of in-the-moment energy, and I think for the first time I understood what it meant to be a real musician." Alex is indeed a musician—and a talented one. He majored in music at Bates College and has mastered the guitar, the sitar, and the Middle Eastern instrument favored by Hamza El Din, the oud.

I've been retired from the music business for many years and now live in rural Maine, distanced from the music industry's front lines. Nevertheless, music remains a huge part of my life. I no longer club-crawl through New York City in search of music, as I did in the early days of my career, but I stay current and have been pleased to find a vibrant and diverse music scene where I live. Many of my friends and neighbors are talented and accomplished musicians who play not to become rich and famous but for the sheer joy of it. When they meet at my house to eat, play, and sing, we are expressing and celebrating life's joys just as my Italian family did when I was a young boy. I am even taking piano lessons again, but this time with a teacher who is nurturing my own pure love of music. Have I come full circle? I like to think of playing music as a spiral—that beautiful form that is ever-present in nature, sinuous and eternally open-ended.

There's a saying:

"Every man dies twice.
First, when the last breath leaves his body,
And second, when his name is spoken for the last time."

This book is my attempt to keep alive many talented people and their stories and preserve the spirit of a unique time in American musical history.

It is both my humble gift and my personal reward.

# ACKNOWLEDGMENTS

# My gratitude and thanks to so many!

| | |
|---|---|
| ALEX BUSHE | an extraordinary young man, whose constant interest and encouragement got me started on this writing adventure |
| STEPHEN ABNEY | my co-writer and patient, loyal friend, who seemed to share my brain, capture my sentiments, reshape and vitalize my drafts, and delight my sense of humor |
| LAUREN BAILEY | my tireless, steadfast, and invaluable editor, whose confidence in me from day one spurred me on to continue this project |
| TIM NASON | who arranged the words on the pages and made my files and notes look like a real book |
| MARK GREENBAUM | an extraordinarily talented artist who saw my vision for the cover before I did |
| DAVID GRISMAN | for making my life richer with his friendship and music |
| MARTY BALIN | for his generous friendship, for opening my doors of perception, and for his gift of song |
| DAVID BROWNE | for not treating me like a man out of time |
| THE EXTRAORDINARY MUSICAL ARTISTS OF THE 60s, 70s, AND 80s | without whom I would have no stories and whose music brought me great joy and helped to define me |
| THE UNIVERSE | for providing |

ROD ROBILLIARD — who so generously gave his time, and whose, interest, encouragement, enthusiasm, comments, critiques, and suggestions helped shape this book

JACKY SARTI — a treasured friend who dropped everything in her life to read the ARC copy of my book with the greatest enthusiasm, a keen eye for detail, and a talent to see things I did not see myself

BETH AND GARY LAWLESS — the owners of Gulf of Maine Books in Brunswick, Maine, who have been a guiding force in a book world I know little about, sharing their knowledge, enthusiasm and encouragement

DEBORAH LANG — my partner in love and life whose selfless contributions to the book leave an indelible mark on its pages and whose spirit brightens my world and my very being

My appreciation and thanks go out to all the exceptional rock 'n' roll chroniclers whose exemplary writing and thoughtful analysis through the years have provided me with hours of enriching entertainment, with a special tip of my hat to Nick Bromell, David Browne, Stephen Davis, Ben Fong-Torres, David Gans, Mikal Gilmore, Robert Greenfield, Blair Jackson, Greil Marcus, Dennis McNally, Joel Selvin, Jeff Tamarkin, and Paul Williams.

I am grateful to all the artists who have written memoirs, generously sharing their lives, with a special nod to John Densmore, Bob Dylan, Levon Helm, Al Kooper, Phil Lesh, Jerry Lee Lewis, Ray Manzarek, Keith Richards, Suze Rotolo, Ellen Sanders, Grace Slick, and Dave Von Ronk.

An additional thank-you to members of Jefferson Airplane, The Doors, the Chambers Brothers, the Rowan Brothers, the Garcia-Saunders Band, the Jerry Garcia Bands, Old and in the Way, and the Grateful Dead, as well as to Robert Hunter, John Barlow, Paul Krassner, Bill Thompson, Sue Stephens, and Alan Trist.

My *High Notes* Support Team continues to be a gift. Thank you all for your unwavering support, for enduring my endless, obsessive book raves, for reading, contemplating, talking things over, being honest, offering comments, and bolstering my confidence: Tom Bailey, David Barth, David Begin, Anne and Dennis Bushe, Jack Casady, Lloyd Chrein, Amy Edelman, Susan Geier, Claire Giachino, the Giachino family, Ann Haight, David Hellman, Karen and Tom Hill, Jorma Kaukonen, Lock Kiermaier, Michael Krassner, Allan Labos, Warren Leight, Phil Lesh, Chuck Lindholm, Susan Mason, Rosie McGee, Laura and Mark Morehouse, My Lebanese Girlfriend, Phil Paone, John Pranio, Randy Sarti, John Scher, Sandy, Erin and Kate at Smith Publicity, Craig Williamson, Stan Smith, Elaine Lanmon, Susan Pink, and Debbye Butler.

On a final *high* note, I extend my apologies to anyone whose name I inadvertently forgot to mention. It does not mean you are any less appreciated, and I thank you too.